Management and Administration
of
Drug and Alcohol Programs

Management and Administration
of
Drug and Alcohol Programs

By

MARVIN D. FEIT, Ph.D., M.Sci.Hyg.

Assistant Professor
University of Tennessee School of Social Work
Assistant Clinical Professor
Department of Psychiatry
University of Tennessee Center for the Health Sciences
Memphis, Tennessee

With a Foreword by

David H. Knott, M.D., Ph.D.

Medical Director
Alcohol and Drug Dependence Clinic
Memphis Mental Health Institute
Assistant Superintendent for Research and Training
Memphis Mental Health Institute
Clinical Associate Professor
Department of Psychiatry
University of Tennessee Center for the Health Sciences
Memphis, Tennessee

CHARLES C THOMAS • PUBLISHER
Springfield • Illinois • U.S.A.

Published and Distributed Throughout the World by

CHARLES C THOMAS ● PUBLISHER

Bannerstone House

301-327 East Lawrence Avenue, Springfield, Illinois, U.S.A.

© *1979, by* CHARLES C THOMAS ● PUBLISHER

ISBN 0-398-03873-2

Library of Congress Catalog Card Number: 78-24527

With THOMAS BOOKS *careful attention is given to all details of
manufacturing and design. It is the Publisher's desire to present books that
are satisfactory as to their physical qualities and artistic possibilities and
appropriate for their particular use.* THOMAS BOOKS *will be true to those
laws of quality that assure a good name and good will.*

Printed in the United States of America
V-R-1

Library of Congress Cataloging in Publication Data

Feit, Marvin D.
  Management and administration of drug and alcohol
programs.

  Includes index.
  1. Drug abuse--Treatment--Management.
2. Alcoholism--Treatment--Management. I. Title.
HV5801.F43   658'.91'36229   78-24527
ISBN 0-398-03873-2

to
Risa, Merryl, and Kimberly

FOREWORD

IN less than a decade the medical, psychological, social, legal, and economic sequelae of alcohol and drug use and misuse have received public attention and emphasis which have been long overdue. The logical approach to the solution of these problems has resulted in an altruistic yet often fragmented organizational endeavor along local, state, and federal institutional lines. Established institutions have been expanded; new institutions have been formed. Confusion concerning social versus public health issues has created the need for skillful and well-informed administration. All too frequently alcohol and drug program administrators have graduated from the ranks of health care providers, with the result often being organizational chaos. Because alcohol and drug-related problems address multiple disciplines, e.g. health care delivery system, criminal justice system, and social service system, extraordinary managerial skills are necessary for optimal program performance. In his book *Management and Administration of Drug and Alcohol Programs,* Dr. Feit elucidates in a clear, comprehensive, and pragmatic manner the special areas of interest indigenous to all alcohol and drug programs. Further, Dr. Feit converts sound and proven managerial principles for application to the unique problems extant in the alcohol and drug treatment enterprise, which recognizes and espouses the virtue of "good administration" but which has failed to recognize the importance of the proper selection and training of personnel in this regard. *Management and Administration of Drug and Alcohol Programs* is an essential and welcome contribution to the field; understanding and implementing the concepts of the book should dramatically improve program management so that successful performance can be

vii

based on the science of administration rather than on seren-
dipity.

DAVID H. KNOTT, M.D., PH.D.

PREFACE

FOCUSING on administrative practice in the drug and alcohol field, this book is intended to serve as a practical guide for all personnel in managerial and administrative positions. It offers readers an opportunity to assess continually their administrative behavior in relation to their organizational environment and administrative tasks.

Information is presented from an administrative perspective. The content is concerned primarily with managerial tasks and responsibilities of conducting both drug and alcohol programs and is less concerned with treatment issues. The management of the treatment aspect of these programs, which is normally a major consideration of similar literature in this field, is considered here as one part of the total management perspective.

In order to accomplish this objective, a matrix for self-assessing administrative practice has been developed. After first describing several developments leading to the need for better management, a self-assessment matrix of administrative practice is described in Chapter 3. The matrix helps to organize relevant pieces of knowledge in specific areas, thus forming a basis for one to understand the complexities of contemporary administrative behavior.

It should be emphasized that this book is intended to be utilized by administrators and not to be placed on a shelf to gather dust. Texts on administration frequently go unused, criticized mainly for their lack of actual administrative awareness, which is another reason why this text was written from the view of an administrator.

Chapters 4 through 7 examine several issues of identified administrative responsibility in the areas of social policy, legal issues, planning and fiscal management, and research and evaluation. The intent is to provide administrators with an understanding of the complexities in each area and is not, therefore, designed to be a comprehensive text on the specific subject matter. In certain instances, readers will be directed to other resource material for a more detailed and thorough analysis of a particular issue.

The subject of each chapter is discussed in relation to the organizational environment of administrators. Certain key issues are delineated for analysis in each of the four chapters. This approach is designed to support the major objective of the text and for administrators to accurately assess their own administrative behavior.

The reader should also keep in mind that constant reference is made to the combined nature of managing drug and alcohol programs. The central thesis is that administrators in either program area have to contend with similar issues, and throughout the text examples are taken from issues present in both programs. For example, confidentiality and program planning are issues administrators in both program areas must face. In discussing each issue, examples are drawn from each program area.

Important, too, is that the overwhelming amount of literature in the field concerns the aspects of treatment and the types of programs. There is a relatively miniscule amount of material available in the management and administrative area. Moreover, this material is scattered and usually too obscure to be of value to administrative personnel. Thus, this text brings together information and organizes it for use by managers, administrators, planners, trainers, professionals, and paraprofessionals in improving their own administrative practices.

M.D.F.

ACKNOWLEDGMENTS

MANY people have been helpful throughout the preparation of this book. I would like to thank the administrators, medical directors, counselors, researchers, clients, ex-clients, funders, and professional colleagues with whom I have worked and those who have taken the time to share firsthand experiences with me. I learned a great deal from being a staff member, administrator, consultant, and researcher in community-based, governmental, and private settings. I owe much to Aaron Mann, Toni Williams, and Lougwin West for their assistance in identifying the need for this type of book and to Michael Baizerman who suggested the possibility of publication. I have benefited greatly from the ideas of Kate Mullins, Muammer Cetingok, David Knott, and Harvey Feldman. The patience of Hugh Vaughn, Carl Wilks, and Lois Thomas is greatly appreciated for allowing me to develop my thoughts in their presence. Barbara Davis performed brilliantly in typing the manuscript and served as a model for meeting deadlines. At home, my family provided encouragement.

M.D.F.

CONTENTS

Management and Administration
of
Drug and Alcohol Programs

Chapter 1

INTRODUCTION

COMPETENT management is an important issue in the drug and alcohol field. It comes to the forefront at a time when important questions are being asked and crucial decisions are being made in both the public and private sector with regard to the accountability and the availability of funds, when domestic programs are under particular scrutiny for the results they produce, with program people fully aware of the possible consequences should those results not be viewed favorably by the various publics.

In the drug and alcohol field competent management becomes mandatory if it is to continue as a problem worthy of constant public support. Unfortunately, at this time, competent management is, to a large degree, quite problematic. For example, increased national attention to alcohol and drug problems which resulted in a rapid increase in the number and scope of all types of programs in this field has, at the same time, created a void in the available number of adequately trained administrators.

Present methods of preparing people for administrative positions also contribute to the need for better management. Administrators in this field usually rise through the programs. They receive management courses only after they are in management positions, and these courses are normally directed toward doing a better job or doing the job the way a funding source would like it to be done. These courses are typically short term and may be more characteristically described as training programs.

Many administrators are also in management positions by virtue of professional achievement. For example, many physicians find themselves on top or near the top in organizational management by virtue of the fact that a program has medical components, and not at all due to their administrative competence. Indeed, for most it probably is or was their first time serving in such a capacity.

These two predominate types of administrators in the drug and alcohol field are therefore at a disadvantage in the world of formal organization and bureaucracy. Neither type has had formal training or education in administration, nor do they typically possess an extensive background in management. Today's administrators have learned their job in the most difficult manner and under some peculiar circumstances.

The major issue concerning management has more to do with producing a constant source of competent administrators for the field and with improving present administrators than with being highly critical about the past. The field does possess competent administrators, but the development of competent managerial personnel simply cannot be left to present methods. Present educational programs in universities focus almost entirely on treatment perspectives and devote little time to the changing scope of administrative responsibilities. This is a glaring deficiency which needs to be rectified.

The practice of administration has changed.[1] Administrators must now possess extensive knowledge in an extremely wide range of areas. In slightly more than a decade the field of administration in human service organizations has changed drastically. For example, program competence must continually be displayed in such content areas as fiscal management, contract development and monitoring, evaluation research, program planning, program development, treatment modalities, policy development, management information systems, personnel policies, affirmative action, interorganizational relations, public relations, staff development, staff training, physical design, space requirements, consultation, and interdisciplinary collaboration. This was not the case about ten years ago.

Administrative training in the drug and alcohol field has not been able to keep pace with the growth of administrative responsibilities. Training programs can effectively serve to orient

---

[1]*See*, for example, Slavin, Simon (Ed.): *Social Administration: The Management of the Social Services.* New York, Haworth, 1978.

people to a particular method or instruct them how to implement a system, but they are limited in providing the understanding and background necessary for appropriate decision-making. People trained in one methodology tend to use it in all other instances. It is probably more useful to provide people with a knowledge base and help them turn it into action than it is to provide them with pre-packaged solutions.

The available literature is usually not accessible to or highly appropriate for administrators. Individual efforts to consolidate the expanding management literature tend to meet much difficulty. The overwhelming majority of new and existing literature is concentrated either on the biological, chemical, social, or legal aspects of alcohol or drugs or on the rehabilitative or treatment aspects of alcohol or drug dependence. A cursory review of current bookshelves, newsletters, journals, and book lists will show this to be accurate. For example, Estes and Heinemann discuss alcohol in relation to developmental aspects, pathophysiological effects, problems in special groups, and therapeutic approaches.[2] Management is not included. Schecter examined the various approaches used in the rehabilitation of drug dependent persons.[3] Management considerations are implied but never discussed fully.

Other literature, which does focus on management, is either program specific or addresses the field of alcohol and drugs separately. Schramm described the development of an employee alcoholism program in industry,[4] and Glatt reviewed innovative techniques in the management of addiction.[5] The complexities of contemporary administration of conventional or merged drug and alcohol programs are rarely discussed in the literature. The available literature is scattered and obscure, further

[2]Estes, Nada J. and Heineman, M. Edith (Eds.): *Alcoholism: Development, Consequences, and Interventions.* St. Louis, Mosby, 1977.

[3]Schecter, Arnold (Ed.): *Rehabilitation Aspects of Drug Dependence.* Cleveland, CRC Press, 1977.

[4]Schramm, Carl J.: Development of a successful alcoholism facility. In Schramm, Carl J. (Ed.): *Alcoholism and Its Treatment in Industry.* Baltimore, Johns Hopkins, 1977, pp. 138-155.

[5]Glatt, Max M. (Ed.): *Drug Dependence: Current Problems and Issues.* Baltimore, University Park, 1977.

hampering the development of competent management.

It is exceedingly difficult to keep pace with the expanding knowledge of the field of administration and the requirements of the changing drug and alcohol field without assistance. It is even more difficult to apply administrative knowledge to one's own practice without appropriate educational supports. The idea of working alone does have merit as an important educational principle and is realistic in relation to the unique conditions of any organization. However, it still remains crucial for administrators to know considerably more than being trained in how to get things done.

Administrators, as heads of organizations, are by definition accountable for all situations and decisions. They are expected by others in the organization to provide direction and guidance. It is therefore important for them to know why they are doing something and be able to explain it, as well as informing and telling people how it might be done. Indeed, understanding the rationale for doing something often provides one with the flexibility to do a better job.

The term administrator is used throughout the text and is intended to cover the broad spectrum of administrative, managerial, supervisory, and executive director personnel. The guiding principle is that each type is in some way directly responsible for the operation of an organization, their organizational position implies certain decision-making responsibilities, and they control the activities of staff. In addition, all four administrative types usually have to address the same issues presented here, with the full recognition that variation does exist in regard to the intensity and the importance of certain tasks. For example, supervisors would be expected to be more concerned with case management issues, while executives would concentrate more on funding issues. But these distinctions can be accounted for in the self-assessment matrix and, hence, are seen as supporting the use of this broad definition of administrator.

In summary, the need for competent management in the drug and alcohol field is increasing and highly consistent with the push for more public accountability. This need comes at a time when present methods for preparing administrative personnel need improvement, and when the relatively small amount of available management literature is obscure and not easily accessible.

Chapter 2

THE NEED FOR BETTER MANAGEMENT

SEVERAL developments have contributed to the need for better management in the drug and alcohol field. The increase in national attention, the uniqueness of the drug and alcohol field, the influx of large sums of money and the expansion of programs, the spread of drugs through many segments of the community, the licensing and credentialing efforts, the professional and paraprofessional struggle, and the expanding scope of administrative responsibility are some factors providing a historical background influencing the development of management in this field.

HISTORICAL PERSPECTIVES

It seems appropriate to describe the historical dimensions of the combined drug and alcohol field. First, the latest increase in national attention is a recent concern, starting in the mid 1960s. Specifically, in 1963 and 1965 federally initiated mental health planning included attention to alcoholism in many states as part of their development of a state comprehensive mental health plan. President Lyndon B. Johnson, in March, 1966, made extensive references to alcoholism in his health and education message. In his speech he made specific references to treating alcoholism as a disease and not a crime.

About the same time, Doctors Dole and Nyswander were utilizing methadone as a therapeutic tool in the rehabilitation of the street addict in New York City. Their published findings gave promise to the rather bleak aspect of rehabilitating drug or heroin addicts.[1]

---

[1]Dole, Vincent P. and Nyswander, Marie E.: Rehabilitation of the street addict. *Archives of Environmental Health, 14*:477-480, 1967; and Dole, Vincent P. and Nyswander, Marie E.: Rehabilitation of heroin addicts after blockade with methadone. *New York Journal of Medicine, 55*:2011-2017, 1966.

In 1966, Congress established a new national policy for the treatment of narcotic addicts. The Narcotic Addict Rehabilitation Act (Public Law 89-793) was signed into law on November 8, 1966, and provided for the civil commitment and treatment of narcotic addicts, including those charged with or convicted of violating certain federal criminal laws. The shift in policy was toward the view that narcotic addiction was symptomatic of an illness to be treated and not a criminal offense in itself.

The necessary groundwork was then laid for a treatment explosion in the drug and alcohol field. Indeed, the rise borders on the spectacular, continually fed by increased media and public attention, presidential pronouncements in the early 1970s regarding drug abuse as the major social problem, congressional action, and the creation of the National Institutes of Alcohol and Alcohol Abuse (NIAAA) and Drug Abuse (NIDA), among several other developments.

The growth of services and treatment programs for alcoholics serves as an example of this explosion. Plaut[2] and Cross[3] document this growth, showing that it paralleled increases in federal and state expenditures needed to support the rapidly expanding services and programs. Cahn also clearly illustrates this thrust.[4] He points out that by the end of 1965, there were approximately twenty-five specialized wards for alcoholic patients in all the state mental hospitals in the United States and another ten to fifteen hospitals without specialized wards but with some sort of specialized program for alcoholic patients, whereas only twenty years before there was only one known specialized ward in all state mental hospitals.[5]

It should be noted that concern for drug abuse was concomitant with the spread of drugs and heroin to more typically

---

[2]Plaut, Thomas E.A.: *Alcohol Problems: A Report to the Nation by the Cooperative Commission on the Study of Alcoholism.* New York, Oxford, 1967.

[3]Cross, Jay N.: *Guide to the Community Control of Alcoholism.* New York, Public Health Association, 1968.

[4]Cahn, Sidney: *The Treatment of Alcoholics.* New York, Oxford, 1970, pp. 67-148.

[5]Cahn, *Treatment of Alcoholics,* p. 72.

[6]Louria, Donald B.: The current heroin situation in the United States. *World Medical Journal, 17*:33-35, 1970; and Boeth, Richard: The heroin plague. *Newsweek,* July 5, 1971, pp. 27-32.

middle class and suburban communities.[6] Legislators on every level were made painfully aware by their constituents of the necessity to *do something about this problem.* In some instances, legislators and their families were directly affected by the drug epidemic. The problem was now pervasive, touching the voting populace, as it grew out of the inner city ghettos and into white America.

An even greater development and expansion of alcoholic treatment programs and services has occurred with regard to community-based and community-oriented facilities. There was thus a rapid growth of outpatient clinics and community mental health centers in the latter half of the 1960s. Plaut indicates that by the first half of the 1970s there were more than 130 outpatient alcoholism clinics and about 2,000 outpatient psychiatric clinics.[7]

In the drug or heroin treatment area, the explosion was probably more like a volcano. Alcohol treatment had for over half a century been in the limelight, and alcohol was decidedly a drug of preference for most abusers. Alcohol was also socially acceptable, meaning that it was readily accessible, prevalent, relatively inexpensive, had considerably less legal complications, and was easy to observe in all walks of life despite it being a socially taboo subject of discussion.

The heroin treatment picture is quite different. As *Newsweek* noted in an article in the summer of 1971 on the heroin plague, "ten years ago, even three years ago, heroin was a loser's drug . . . For years the official figure was pegged at 68,000 addicts, but neither the Federal government nor any private agency knew if this estimate was even close — nor did they care as long as the heroin users stayed out of sight."[8] Heroin addiction was considered a problem below the threshhold of social concern, at least until the 1970s.

While official figures in regard to the total population of heroin addicts in the country vary, no one disputes the fact that many more people entered treatment facilities in the 1970s than ever before in American history. *Newsweek* estimated that

[7]Plaut, *Alcohol Problems*, pp. 53-85.
[8]Boeth, Newsweek, p. 27.

about 2,500 treatment centers of one kind or another existed by 1975.[9] In the same year, belief that heroin addiction among United States Armed Forces personnel in Vietnam was at crisis proportions forced massive programs to be launched by the Army.

One need not be deluded into thinking that this alcohol and drug growth was or is a temporary phenomenon. According to the NIAAA, about one in ten of the almost 100 million who drink is now either a full-fledged alcoholic or at least a problem drinker, defined by NIAAA as one who drinks enough to cause trouble for himself and society.[10] Moreover, from 1960 to 1970, per capita consumption of alcohol in the United States increased 25 percent, to the equivalent of 2.6 gallons of straight alcohol per adult per year.[11] Quoting Doctor Morris Chafetz, then director of the Department of Health, Education and Welfare's NIAAA, "Youths are moving from a wide range of drugs to the most devastating drug — the one most widely misused of all — alcohol."[12]

Demonstrating that similarities exist between alcohol and drug abusers naturally suggests an ever increasing pool of abusers eligible for treatment. Not only are the separate lines for *alcohol* and/or *drug* treatment blurred, but there is a new category added, the *polydrug* user/abuser. In essence, the target population as seen by officials is and would continue to be increasing both in size and seriousness of the abuse syndrome. Thus, the number of treatment programs today remains quite high despite having reached a plateau by the mid 1970s.

UNIQUENESS OF THE DRUG AND ALCOHOL FIELD

The drug and alcohol field is unique, for it is intimately connected to the much larger and even more complex health and medical field and to the highly political and emotional social welfare field. On one hand administrators must make

---

[9]Boeth, *Newsweek*, p. 31.
[10]Alcoholism: New victims, new treatment. *Time*, April 22, 1974, pp. 75-81.
[11]Alcoholism, *Time*, p. 75.
[12]Alcoholism, *Time*, p. 75.

program decisions in relation to the physicians involved in their programs. These physicians are part of the health and medical care delivery system, which operates like no other system in this country. For example, physicians alone determine the course of medical treatment and decide what diagnostic tests are needed. Physician costs are set by the provider and not by the market principle of supply and demand. Quite often patients or clients do not know the cost of the service provided, as reimbursement usually comes from third-party insurance mechanisms.

On the other hand, administrators must also consider how their decisions would be viewed in the context of domestic social programming. In this area they must compete with a host of other social problems for available funds and the public's shifting attitude toward drug and alcohol users. Scientific input usually is mitigated against political considerations in reaching funding and programming decisions, with the drug and alcohol field often considered as to how it impacts on other socially important problems of the day, such as crime in the streets and domestic violence.

The relationship of the drug and alcohol field to the two larger fields of health care and social welfare add immeasurably to the difficulty of effectively managing programs. Relationships have to be maintained with representatives of the larger fields, their issues have to be analyzed as to their impact on drug and alcohol issues, and a delicate balance has to be maintained between their sometimes inconsistent and conflicting views.

THE INCREASE IN AVAILABLE FUNDS

The rapid increase in drug and alcohol treatment programs has naturally created a need for a substantial base of supervisory, management, and administrative personnel. Prior to program expansion there had been relatively few people working in this area, and little attention had been devoted to the problems encountered in conducting drug and alcohol rehabilitation programs. Also, the two fields of drugs and alcohol were indeed separate entities with practically no opportunity for communication between them. This perspective has changed to some degree, with the absolute number of people working on all levels in these two fields now being quite large, particularly in positions at the management or administrative level.

It is fairly easy to predict that a lag would develop between the availability of management and administrative positions and the number of adequately prepared personnel to fill those positions during the years of rapid expansion. Yet, despite its recognition, little has been accomplished which moves toward alleviating the overall problem, and the managerial problems persist. There are additional dimensions the impact of increased availability of funds had on the management situation which are important to emphasize.

The field of drug and alcohol treatment itself was not originally a glamorous one. Consequently, few professional people were drawn to work with drug addicts or alcoholics. Also, the field was quite small, had relatively few dollars, and, hence, did not offer very favorable job opportunities. The reported *success* or *cure* rate was abysmally low, so one working in the field was often faced with frustration. All in all, drug and alcohol treatment was not very high on the inventory of interesting social problems to which the helping professions desired to address.

When the influx of federal dollars made jobs plentiful, there was a sudden discovery and importance attached to finding employment in the field. Furthermore, methadone treatment provided guarded optimism that rehabilitation of the street heroin addict was possible. Hope abounded that rehabilitation of the street heroin addict and the chronic alcoholic was within the grasp of professional and paraprofessional intervention.

Unfortunately, one cannot overlook the impact of race in the overall situation. The drug or *heroin* problem was now spreading into the suburbs. Crime was attached to the drug problem specifically through such slogans as *law and order* and *make our streets safe at night*. Publicity continued to throw the spotlight on heroin as the major factor in crime and a wide range of urban ills. Thus, despite how one examines the situation, it is painfully clear that while politicians, governmental officials, and others did finally act on the overall situation, one of the most potent factors causing this action was simply because whites were now being directly and indirectly affected at ever increasing and alarming rates by drug-related problems.

In the struggle for employment, the issue of who could best treat program participants was of major importance. The notion that ex-addicts, ex-alcoholics, and people in treatment could more effectively provide treatment became highly popular, and people in these categories competed with professionals for jobs. The issue still rages and may never be resolved, in part because it is phrased so as to provide no answers. For example, professionals or paraprofessionals are categories primarily describing the educational level of a person, whereas the attributes and skills which make for a better helper or worker are not mutually exclusive. Hence, the issue of overlap between both categories in the ability of their members to help is never really addressed.

THE CREDENTIALING EFFORT

One force looms important in the employment issue. The funding sources, implementing or at least representing society's perspective, had to move ultimately in the direction of legitimizing or institutionalizing the workers in the field. This legitimation has taken the form of licensing, credentialing, or providing educational and training opportunities primarily for paraprofessionals and, to a much less extent, for professionals.

There is no doubt that the focus on this legitimizing effort has been the counselor or the one working directly with the program participant. Reasons for this approach appear logical in that since one is striving for better service or treatment to clients one should start at the level of worker and client interaction.

There also seems to be another reason for focusing on the counselor. Practically all of the other personnel in the field already had been licensed. In methadone centers, for example, nurses, physicians, social workers, psychologists, pharmacists, and other professionals had degrees showing they had the necessary educational credentials. Moreover, professionals were more likely to be found in administrative or supervisory positions.

After all, the funding sources respond to credentialed personnel. A major assumption was made that these people were capable, spoke the same language, and had the requisite skills for the position by virtue of their educational achievements. The difficulty with this assumption in the drug and alcohol field is that it is not always accurate, particularly in the drug-related part of the combined field.

While much the same case could be made for the field of alcohol treatment, there are some important differences. Treatment programs had been in operation for many more years and had already involved paraprofessionals or ex-drinkers in their service regimen. Quite often this aspect of treatment was delivered by a recovered alcoholic or someone from Alcoholics Anonymous, so nearly everyone in alcohol treatment programs had experience with nonprofessionals providing some form of treatment.

In addition, this already functioning nonprofessional group often served as a counterbalancing force retarding the invasion of other nonprofessionals. It could often serve as a rather formidable opponent by naturally being expected to keep control of the *prized* position it already possessed. The notions of territorial imperative and ownership of turf therefore emerge in this atmosphere. In the drug field this hierarchical alignment of paraprofessional personnel was amorphous and up for grabs.

An obvious and almost inescapable conclusion thus emerges. The thrust to license counselors, particularly paraprofessionals, was easier to develop rather than confront professionals with their lack of understanding of the many problems inherent in administering programs and in providing treatment. Politically, and logically, the best route was to train the group with the least clout, such as the paraprofessional, the nonprofessional, the ex-addict, or however one chooses to describe people in this field lacking educational and professional degrees.

The administrative picture should now be much clearer. Individuals with professional degrees were able to find gainful employment on a management level in a flourishing field, which had received national attention, money, and a renewed hope for successful rehabilitative efforts. In the rush, most found themselves in management positions for which they were not trained, with a host of rehabilitative problems which did not budge or go away simply by their presence and despite their efforts.

The difficult situation of a professional learning about administrative responsibilities on the job was prevalent during this explosion period. To be sure, many professionals assumed administrative tasks without difficulty and did outstanding jobs. In the main, however, it became painfully clear to federal and state funding source representatives, many professionals, program participants, and just about everyone in the entire treatment system that administrators and managers could profit by programs designed to increase their administrative practice. The most common learning methods, on-the-job training and trial and error, left much to be desired.

The time has come for additional learning methods to be used to prepare administrators. Educationally oriented programs can more easily be directed toward developing competence in managing the complex nature of drug and alcohol programs. The present system is much too fragmented and poorly developed to keep pace with the changing scope of administration. Educationally oriented programs in administration are also needed to substantially augment the current patchwork method of selecting administrators.

The need for developing education-oriented programs does not minimize the continued necessity for learning on-the-job, which is particularly important in the unique drug and alcohol field, but it does raise some very important questions relative to who is or is not capable of managing programs. Educationally oriented programs can attract people with perhaps innovative ideas who would not normally have access into managerial positions. These people could help direct programs and respond to program needs from an administrative perspective, while allowing treatment people time to concentrate on their job.

Many educational institutions have incorporated alcohol and drug abuse material into their curriculums. However, this material is practically all geared toward treatment or service organization perspectives. There is virtually nothing in curriculums which pertains to administering drug and alcohol programs.

The educational institutions are themselves at a point where they could benefit greatly by a reassessment of the drug and alcohol field. For example, only recently have drugs and alcohol been considered as a single entity. It does not take long to observe the ambivalence in every aspect and level of this field in regard to viewing drugs and alcohol as separate fields or as one field. Thus, on one hand, one may view the emergence of single state agencies and the development of chemical dependency or substance abuse curriculums in universities as attempts toward unifying the field. At the same time, one is able to observe the perpetuation of separate fields by the continuation of separate references to drugs and alcohol and the separate national institutes (NIAAA and NIDA) with their separate funding bases.

There is a paucity of material dealing with the scope of an administrator's task in the context of drug and alcohol programs. The dimensions of this problem are extensive. Administrators are being asked or required to be planners, fund-raisers, experts in third-party reimbursement mechanisms, program assessors, evaluators, and negotiators and to perform many other functions in the course of managing their programs. Dwindling funds make it impossible to hire specialized staff and, in some cases, consultants to do some of these tasks. The result is often that an administrator has very little support in these key management areas and must complete many tasks with little or no help. Consequently, each agency reviewing any such material is likely to criticize the administrative component of the program. Stated simply, an administrator cannot be all things to all people and be expected to do everything well, yet this is precisely the situation in which administrators in this field often find themselves.

In summation, the need for better management has developed from many perspectives. The rapid expansion in available funds brought in many people and created administrative positions, without providing the necessary supports for competent management. New and different methods of preparing administrators are called for as present methods are inadequate. Complicating the development of educationally oriented methods of instruction is the paucity of available literature. The available literature is fragmented and therefore does not provide a comprehensive view of the managerial aspects of administration, such as legal, policy, planning, fiscal, research, and evaluation aspects, which are discussed in the next four chapters.

Chapter 3

SELF-ASSESSMENT MATRIX FOR ADMINISTRATIVE PRACTICE

THE self-assessment matrix for administrative practice is presented as a method for administrators to evaluate their skill and competence in the process of making decisions. It is practice-oriented and when used regularly can provide a clear perspective of one's own strengths and weaknesses. The matrix is self-administered, becoming easier and more flexible with use and normally requiring a short period of analytic thought before acting.

The matrix is a technique for organizing and categorizing administrative behavior. It is a way to pare many faceted problems into manageable parts, so that tasks such as the securing of grant funds can proceed more orderly and with greater insight regarding division of labor among staff. It also is useful to managers who would like to know what to expect, since the matrix can be used to speculate on the responses of various people and organizations to their own decisions and their responses to decisions by other people and other organizations.

SELF-ASSESSMENT MATRIX

The self-assessment matrix has two components. The first component may be called the administrative task, and the second component may be called the systems of administration (*see* Fig. 1).

As Figure 1 suggests, the arrangement of these two components in a grid or matrix pattern has the distinct advantage of locating properly one or more managerial problems occurring simultaneously. In this way, administrators can pinpoint both the task area which seems to be problematic and its system context. Administrators would thus no longer accept a problem

ADMINISTRATIVE TASK	THE SYSTEMS OF ADMINISTRATION				
	General	Organization	Organization Unit	Organization Unit-Individual Specific	Inter-Intrapersonal
Policy					
Legal					
Planning and Fiscal Management					
Research and Evaluation					

Figure 1. The Self-Assessment Matrix of Administrative Practice.

statement such as *this is a policy problem,* but rather relate the *policy* problem to one or more of the organizational systems. For example, an administrator may find local policy on hiring ex-addicts to be fairly clear and federal policy to be conflicting and vague. One advantage, therefore, would be for an administrator to more precisely locate the source of the policy problem, which should also provide one with a clearer idea of how to proceed.

DEFINING THE COMPONENTS

The Administrative Tasks

It is important to understand the two components of the self-assessment matrix. The administrative task component is subdivided into four major categories of managerial responsibility. The policy category is seen as encompassing the rules and regulations which apply to people and programs in general. Personnel policies, medical and social treatment protocols, federal and state directives, affirmative action guidelines, and regulations appearing in the Federal Register would be included in the policy category.

The legal category would encompass all issues and concerns related to law and the criminal justice system. While one obvious consideration in this category has to do with client contact in the court, some other content areas would be client confidentiality, the rights of program participants, the protection of human subjects in research, and malpractice. In addition, organizational issues pertaining to the tax code, workmen's compensation, unemployment compensation, the emergence of labor unions, nonprofit corporate law, personnel law, entering contract for service arrangements, and legislation before the various federal, state, county, and city governments would be included.

Planning would account for those activities which establish a conscious attempt to solve problems or direct future actions.[1]

---

[1]Gilbert, Neil and Specht, Harry: *Planning for Social Welfare.* Englewood Cliffs, N.J., Prentice-Hall, 1977, p. 1.

Foremost in this category is the plan developed by programs for new or continued programming efforts, the county or local drug and alcohol plan, and the state drug and alcohol plan. Fiscal planning, the planning of information systems, the establishment of treatment referral relationships between service organizations, public relations efforts, program planning, and, in effect, the process by which similar tasks are addressed also belong in the planning category.

The fourth category is research and evaluation. The type of activities in this category are those which are intended to answer questions raised in the program or in the field about the client population and the organizations themselves. The intent of research would be to raise questions and then devise a systematic method for their investigation, such as which treatment method works best with what clients, or to learn what types of clients have the lowest recidivism rate. Evaluation studies would be geared toward placing a value on specific program efforts or on the whole program itself. Such type studies as single subject, case study, and program research would be part of this category.

The distinctions between the four categories of administrative responsibility and their related tasks are intended to provide administrators with a useful way of organizing their information about problems they encounter. Most organizational issues or problems are expected to cut across more than one administrative task category, but will also vary in impact and intensity according to its system context. For example, assume that staff development is an issue on which there are many different views. Using the category approach just described, an administrator would minimally consider (1) whether or not policies existed in the agency or in other agencies, and, if so, what is stated in the policies; (2) any legal implications, such as whether the use of funds for staff development would be consistent with existing contracts or agreements; (3) the best organized effort, or plan, for the implementation of staff development activities; and (4) whether any evidence exists demonstrating the value or worth of such a staff program effort. In essence, one would be able to obtain a greater degree of precision about the staff development issue and could easily determine the type of administrative work which lies ahead.

The same analytical technique is used to assist administrators in making distinctions in the systems of administration component of the matrix. The organizational position of administrators will be viewed in the context of the various subsystems in which it is located.

System Characteristics

Since the concept *system* is used extensively in the matrix it seems imperative that attention is focused on its characteristics. These characteristics are important because they enable one to build a bridge between social systems theory and the particular administrative problems posed in practice.

The kind of systems of prime interest in this analysis may be defined as a complex of elements tied together in a network and related in a specific manner, such that the relationship of each element and the corresponding patterns of interaction are relatively stable at and within any period of time.[2] The elements may exist in any form. They may be "relatively simple and stable or complex and changing . . . the interrelations between them may be mutual or unidirectional, linear, non-linear or intermittent, and varying in degrees of causal efficacy or priority."[3]

This definition of systems suggests some of the major characteristics: A social system is composed of elements, these elements are interrelated, and a pattern of interaction exists between the elements. Further analysis suggests additional important characteristics, such as a tendency toward equilibrium, its degree of openness, an alteration or change in any part of the system affects all other parts, and that feedback is particularly important to its operation and maintenance.

COMPOSED OF ELEMENTS. An element is defined as one of the constituent parts of some larger whole. As such it may be seen as the unit of analysis employed in explaining interaction from

---

[2]Hall, A. D. and Fagen, R. E.: Definitions of systems. *General Systems Yearbook*, 1:13-28, 1956.
[3]Buckley, Walter: *Sociology and Modern Systems Theory*. Englewood Cliffs, N.J., Prentice-Hall, 1967, p. 41.

the point of view of a given discipline.[4] In this book, for example, a therapeutic system would minimally consist of a patient, a therapist, and a host agency. Each part would be defined as an element.

INTERRELATEDNESS OF THE ELEMENTS. The constituent elements operate in a manner that tends to bind them together. They fundamentally need each other to exist, without which there can be no system. In the therapeutic system of a patient, a therapist, and a host agency, the system only becomes operative the moment an individual asks a therapist for help. Without this basic act, the system does not exist. The moment any element in the therapeutic system withdraws, the system also ceases to exist. Use of the concept system by definition implies an interrelatedness among the elements, although at times the degree of interrelatedness may vary.

PATTERNS OF INTERACTION. Patterns of interaction are those behaviors exhibited by the elements in the system which, over a period of time, begin to show a certain degree of regularity. These behaviors often become the norms[5] which provide the elements of a system with the justification, idealization, and realization of its functions and a common acceptance of the rules to get the job done.[6] These norms then provide a hold on the elements and form the basis for identifying specific behaviors, such as expectations and deviancy.

In Parsonian terms the pattern of interaction is probably similar to his concept of order. Parsons and Shils define the notion of system in relation to this concept: "The most general and fundamental property of a system is the interdependence of parts or variables. Interdependence consists in the existence of determinate relationship among the parts or variable as contrasted with randomness of variability. In other words interdependence is *order* in the relationship among the components

---

[4]Loomis, Charles P.: *Social Systems: Essays on Their Persistence and Change.* New York, Van Nostrand, 1960, pp. 5-6.

[5]Loomis, *Social Systems,* pp. 16-19.

[6]Polsky, Howard: System as patient: Client needs and system function. In Hearn, Gordon (Ed.): *The General Systems Approach: Contributions Toward an Holistic Conception of Social Work.* New York, Council on Social Work Education, 1969, p. 13.

which center into a system."[7]

TENDENCY TOWARD EQUILIBRIUM. The patterns of interaction and the elements exist in a network which tends toward a balance existing between these factors. This means that a natural aspect of a system is for all its elements to move toward establishing a balance by the guidance of norms as a stabilizing factor.[8] Once a new factor is introduced, either internally or externally, the elements will behave in a manner that tends toward either re-establishing the prior balance or establishing a new balance. Both behaviors are indicative of a tendency toward equilibrium.

Buckley's use of the concepts morphogenesis and morphostasis are helpful in understanding the various processes which emerge from a system's tendency toward equilibrium.[9] The latter concept describes those processes which tend to preserve or maintain a given system's form, structure, or state. The former concept describes processes in complex system-environment exchanges that tend to elaborate or change a system's organization, state, or form.

DEGREE OF OPENNESS. Openness refers to that characteristic of a system either influencing or being influenced by the environment as well as by its own elements. A system that is thought to be *closed* is characterized as self-sufficient and autonomous.[10] Open systems are in continual interaction internally and with a constantly changing environment.[11] As a result of this internal-external interaction, the system is in a position to influence or be influenced by other systems, recognizing that the degree of openness may vary within and between systems.

FEEDBACK RESPONSE. Feedback is a form of communication which provides the elements of a system with a way of taking

[7]Parsons, Talcott and Shils, E. A. (Eds.): *Toward a General Theory of Action.* Cambridge, Ma., Harvard, 1951, p. 107.
[8]Parsons, Talcott: *The Social System.* New York, Free Press, 1951.
[9]Buckley, *Sociology and Modern Systems Theory,* pp. 58-66.
[10]Berrien, F. K.: *General and Social Systems.* New Brunswick, N.J., Rutgers Univ. Press, 1968, pp. 15-23.
[11]Bertalanffy, Ludwig von: *General Systems Theory.* San Diego, N.Y., Brazilier, 1968, pp. 42-44; and Buckley, *Sociology and Modern Systems Theory,* pp. 52-55.

in and measuring information.[12] It is often used as a means of stabilizing a certain action, or "for the direction of actions towards a goal where the aberration from the goal is fed back, as information, till the goal or target is reached."[13]

Systems of Administration

In applying systems theory to the role of an administrator in the decision-making process, a temporal sequence is described for analytical purposes. Since all administrators use some form of a temporal sequence or thought process in reaching a decision, the sequence described here is explored in relation to how administrators could apply their knowledge in a systematic manner to the problems they face. Such attempts, while difficult at first, become easier to use when understood and applied. Continued application of this type of analysis should lead to a greater degree of clarity and confidence in outcome by an administrator.

The temporal sequence administrators might be expected to use in reaching decisions is seen in Figure 2.

Three major points about Figure 2 need to be discussed. First, five distinct subsystems emerge for analysis. Second, these subsystems are represented as being on a continuum, and, third, the organizational work unit-individual specific subsystem is where the actions and behaviors of people are clearest.

The five distinct subsystems which emerge for analysis when systems theory is applied to the temporal sequence of administrative decision-making are the general, the organization, the organization unit, the organization unit-individual specific, and the inter-intrapersonal. These subsystems are represented on a continuum primarily because it is improper to place them in a hierarchical order. Such an order would suggest a level or ladder ranking, thereby implying that one subsystem of anal-

---

[12]Bertalanffy, *General Systems Theory,* p. 43.
[13]*See* for example, Churchman, C. West: *The Systems Approach.* New York, Dell, 1968; and Monane, Joseph H.: *A Sociology of Human Systems.* New York, Appleton-Century-Crofts, 1967.

THE FIVE SUBSYSTEMS OF ADMINISTRATION

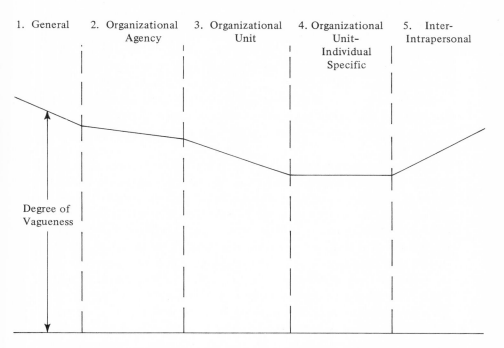

Figure 2. Systems Theory Applied to the Temporal Sequence of Administrative Decision Making.

ysis had to be completed before proceeding to the next or that one was on a higher order or was better than the lower levels. The opposite of ranking is suggested with emphasis placed upon understanding the impact each subsystem has on the other, even when one is called upon to compress or elongate the five subsystems in relation to time. For example, when an administrator learns of information requiring immediate action in subsystem 1, the general system, and must make some assessment of its organizational usefulness, the temporal sequence or thought process is very likely compressed at that moment in time to include the reactions of people inside the organization, as in subsystems 3 and 4. In this way, subsystems 1, 3, and 4 are meshed or closely connected in time.

On the other hand, when an administrator initially plans how useful information is to be incorporated into agency procedures and has considerably less pressure, the same temporal sequence might be stretched in time to include a more detailed assessment of the kind of information available in each subsystem, so that the plan might receive a favorable response from the other workers. Regardless of the many pressures on administration practice, such as time and the accumulation of data, the same temporal sequence would be used in reaching a decision.

The degree of vagueness is least in subsystem 4. As one moves further away from this subsystem, the more vague and abstract becomes the interaction of and between the elements and, consequently, the terms and concepts used to describe the interaction. In subsystem 4, administrators can easily observe the behaviors of individuals in relation to their work unit, whereas in the organization unit subsystem the interaction between members in two or more group units of an organization may be more difficult to observe. When one has to rely on interpretations of behavior and impugn motivation to people, the more likely one is to use terms which tend to be more vague and abstract. Instead of being able to describe the observable behavior, one has to ascribe behavior and its meaning to people, without knowing if it has been placed in its proper context. Thus, psychological labels used to describe intra or interpersonal behavior in subsystem 5 may be as vague as sociological labels used to describe organizational life in the general subsystem or subsystem 1.

The general subsystem is the first subsystem described in the temporal sequence (*see* Fig. 3). It is the subsystem in which project administrators operate where tasks are sometimes not clear and where one can easily get lost in the interorganizational exchanges. This is the macro system of a project administrator and would normally include all aspects affecting organizational life. The administrator's system, for example, would include one's professional national association, similar programs in other states, societal views and attitudes, and the views of Congress and relevant federal agencies.

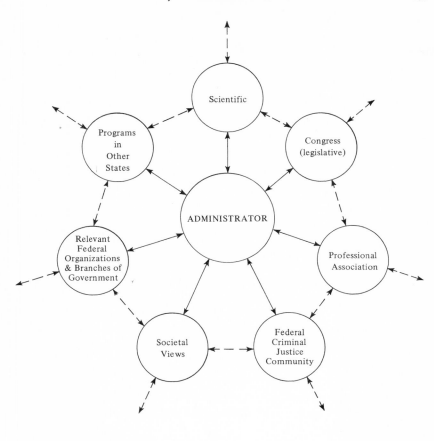

Direct Contact, Visible and Known
Indirect Contact, Generally Invisible and Unknown

Figure 3. General Subsystem of the Administrator.

It is the general subsystem in which an administrator and related elements tend to be farthest removed from each other and to which the activities in and between the elements are rather obscure and abstract. For example, an administrator would not be expected to have a clear understanding of how decisions get made in Congress or when certain legislative activities will occur. An administrator would respond normally to calls for action by specific people or organizations where trust has developed over a period of time.

In the general subsystem, the elements interact usually on their own and with minimum individual administrator input. For example, Congress could be expected to respond to certain societal views regarding drug and alcohol treatment. Certain departments of the federal government could respond to the same concerns, to pressures from the legislative and executive branches, or to both. Subsequent decisions on the federal level often proceed with or without administrator input. As a result of such interaction between elements in the general subsystem, their decisions could and often do impact upon organizational decision making.

It is also the general subsystem in which an astute administrator could ascertain national trends or obtain useful personal and organizational information. In some instances, national conferences are supposed to produce this effect, as is one's participation on national boards or committees. By noticing trends in other parts of the country, for example, one can gain valuable *lead time* in taking various steps within the organization to meet the changing trends. It is an administrator's responsibility to use that time productively, rather than waiting for a decision to be made and then reacting quickly and without much awareness.

It should be noted, however, as Figure 3 suggests, that the type of communication pattern for an administrator is basically one in which administrator interaction with the other elements is limited and in which one usually has little control over events. In these situations individual contact is typically substituted by group or organizational contact, such as when an administrator brings people from other states into his/her organizational situation, when national associations are formed, or when one participates in some legislative activity with people from the scientific community. An administrator mostly controls the extent and frequency of the contact, interaction, and communication with each of these elements, when the contact is predominately self-motivated and self-determined. An administrator is more likely to respond to the requests or the demands of the elements perceived as influential, such as the regulatory groups.

Since the administrator keys or triggers the various interac-

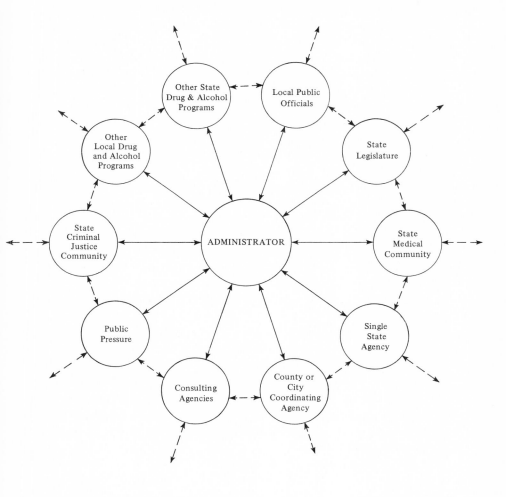

Direct Contact, Visible and Known
Indirect Contact, Generally Invisible and Unknown

Figure 4. Organization Subsystem of the Administrator.

tions, it is important to remember and to readily assume that there will be variation in the extent of involvement with each element. An administrator will communicate and become more involved with some elements and less involved with others. With the process of selection and discrimination operating, the administrator possesses the ability to increase or decrease both the number and extent of involvement with each element of the general subsystem.

The organization system (*see* Fig. 4) is the second subsystem where one can analyze administrators and their more immediate and external environment. In this subsystem administrators can more easily translate the activities of each element into concrete services and regulations directly affecting program operations. It, too, has specific requirements and its own tasks.

The organization subsystem may be characterized by the closeness or immediacy of external organizations to the operations of one's own agency. For example, the agency may be bound to a state organization by virtue of contractual obligations, by direct sign-off for program approval, or for certain operational requirements. Thus, any shift in any immediate external organization's policy, funds, or change in personnel, would be very closely watched for probable internal effects on one's organization.

It is the organization subsystem to which administrators most often have to respond to competing external forces and in which one may feel the most pressure for making certain types of decisions. Quite often the pressure of law enforcement officials, patient advocates, political officials, health department personnel, state government personnel, and other interested groups is acutely felt in decisions regarding patient treatment or program operations.

In the third subsystem of analysis an administrator responds to the agency's internal system. This organization unit subsystem requires a division of the administrator's organization into several distinct and distinguishable units or departments (*see* Fig. 5). These organizational units might minimally include patients, medical personnel, counselors, board of directors, maintenance and clerical staff, and supervisors. Administrators would be expected to interact selectively with each unit or department. For example, administrative work may require more time to be spent with board members, with some departments, or with clients.

The organization unit subsystem implies a higher number of observable behaviors in administrator control than in the pre-

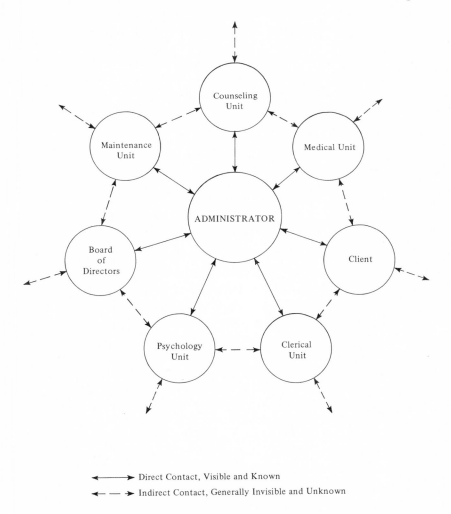

→ Direct Contact, Visible and Known

← — → Indirect Contact, Generally Invisible and Unknown

Figure 5. Organization Unit Subsystem of the Administrator.

vious two subsystems. A detailed pattern of interaction is more easily identified, since daily interactions can be readily seen by the administrator. The types of concerns are also not as abstract as in the previous two subsystems. For example, workers in one department may want to change treatment methods, and they interact with their supervisors on this specific item. These individual or small group behavioral responses to specific problems may be observed readily and monitored on a daily basis by administrators.

This subsystem appears to have a greater degree of direct and observable communication between the elements. This situation would seem to occur evidently because of proximity, i.e. the physical closeness of the elements of the subsystem. In this case, it is more likely for workers in the treatment facility or office to interact and talk among themselves about the behavior of other workers and project clients than with workers in other agencies. Administrators would be privy to information both within the work unit and between work units. This amount of information is not available in the previous two subsystems.

This subsystem also suggests that the frequency of interaction between the elements is on a continual and routine basis. In the general and organization subsystems, the frequency of interaction between an administrator and the elements may be at times very high, but the nature and type of interaction would normally be time limited.

The fourth subsystem is the organization unit-individual specific. An administrator operates in relation to the individuals who comprise a specific unit or department. Individual strengths and weaknesses for addressing unit or agency problems are assessed, such as the division of labor, scapegoating, and individual satisfaction, as illustrated in Figure 6.

It should be easy to recognize that the organization unit-individual specific subsystem can be commonly perceived as encompassing the daily operations of departments and other agency-related units. However, one can also see clearly the importance of understanding people and how they may be expected to respond in particular situations. Administrators must now consider a second aspect of decision making, the human

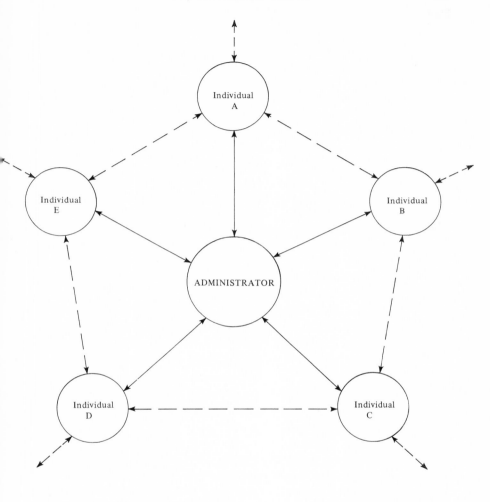

→ Direct Contact, Visible and Known
← — → Indirect Contact, Generally Invisible and Unknown

Figure 6. Organization Unit-Individual Specific Subsystem of the Administrator.

response. The *they* often referred to in organizational behavior becomes an identifiable person. Such people must be considered as individuals in their own right and as group members in the decision-making process, for their responses may differ accordingly.

The organization unit-individual specific subsystem is essential to administrative decision making as it includes identification of points of intervention in solving problems in the broad context and the specifics of how, what, and with whom does one interact in order to get something done. It is at this point that the activities of agency units, supervisors, and administrators become visible, more easily understood, and measureable.

The fifth area of analysis is the inter-intrapersonal subsystem in which the one-on-one situation is addressed (*see* Fig. 7). This subsystem necessitates a shift to a more psychological orientation, since it involves an administrator's assessment of the personal characteristics and the type of individual to whom one must direct attention.

Let us assume for the moment that an administrator has selected some important individuals to assist in the solution of a problem. The extent of administrative success in solving the problem could easily depend on the administrator's understanding of the stability, dependability, motivations, or the psychological makeup of those key individuals. Thus, in this subsystem one would normally ask such questions as, "Can we rely on her?" or "Will Mr. X do this on his own or will he need assistance?"

It is interesting to note the emergence of a paradox. The focus on the specific attributes of individuals in this subsystem, which might at first seem more understandable than concepts used to describe organizational behavior in the general system, instead provides one with the same conceptual abstractness, as there is no greater clarity in understanding concepts used to describe individual behavior. Despite the illusion of specificity, in part fostered by the one-to-one scale, there actually exists the same vagueness in the psychologically oriented concepts and labels applied to understanding interpersonal behavior as has been depicted in the use of sociologically oriented systems jargon.

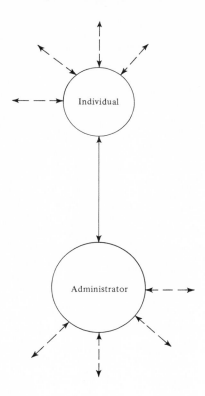

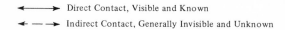

Direct Contact, Visible and Known

Indirect Contact, Generally Invisible and Unknown

Figure 7. Inter-Intrapersonal Subsystem of the Administrator.

In summary, the two subsystems in which administrators have greatest control and influence and where observable and measureable behavioral acts occur on a daily basis are the organization unit and the organization unit-individual specific. These subsystems relate to the internal operations of an agency and are therefore much more tangible. The general and organization subsystems are external to an agency, and an administrator's actions in each tend to be more sporadic, highly intense at certain times, and group or association-oriented. The inter-intrapersonal subsystem is related to the understanding of individual behavior, particularly under certain conditions, and can be applied to individuals in the other four subsystems.

Application of the Matrix

The most useful aspects of the self-assessment matrix have yet to be discussed. At this point the matrix provides excellent insight into understanding the nature of administrative problems, properly identifying and specifying those problems in ways which can offer some possible solutions or their resolution. But this is only one part of the total situation. In order to be more effective, administrators need to know and assess their ability and familiarity with each part of the two components in the matrix. For example, while it is fine to realize that one is confronted with a financial planning problem within an agency, it would be even better to be able to convert the knowledge into action.

As administrators apply the matrix to their practice, they need to rate their experience level with the administrative task and to rate their degree of familiarity with the particular administrative subsystem. When the two ratings are correlated, one is clearly able to assess much about administrative behavior, such as the extent of knowledge, the degree of comfortableness with the perceived or actual problem, the desired method of intervention, and the development of appropriate strategies.

Administrators could use a simple low, medium, and high ranking to rate their own experience level with administrative tasks. A low score would mean little exposure or knowledge of the task and that one has not done it before. A medium score would mean moderate exposure of the task and no experience with it or some experience and little exposure. A high score would indicate that one has a high degree of skill, is well versed in the area, and has done the particular or related task before.

Administrators could assess their own degree of familiarity

with a particular subsystem by ranking themselves either high or low. A low ranking would mean that one does not feel confident about the particular subsystem and needs more data to fill in the knowledge gaps. Obviously, a high ranking would indicate that one feels confident about the knowledge base and the elements of the subsystem.

If self-assessments are properly done according to this method, one should immediately perceive variations occurring in each component aspect of the matrix. An important feature is that just as there will be variations in one component, such as high rankings in policy and planning, low in legal, and medium in research and evaluation, there also will be variations in each task in relation to the five subsystems of administration. Thus, a high ranking in planning may be assessed in the organization unit subsystem, but a low ranking in planning would be assessed in the general subsystem.

An individual, therefore, has two assessments, level of experience and degree of familiarity, to compare in each cell of the matrix. A combined assessment would be obtained from the combination of the two rankings, which would be either low-low, low-medium, low-high, medium, medium-high, or high-high.

This assessment technique may be translated easily into administrative behavior. In areas where one has a low-low or a low-medium ranking, it should be very clear that one must proceed with caution, needs much information, and could probably use outside help. When a medium-high or a high-high ranking occurs, an administrator will probably proceed with much confidence, have well-developed sources of information, and feel as if he/she could have an impact on the outcome of the situation. In low-high rankings, one typically proceeds without a firm base, can easily feel less sure of himself/herself, and may appear unable to reach a decision.

As in all self-assessment procedures, it is possible for people to not rate themselves accurately. The difficulty, however, is not with the procedure but with the people, for they can obtain an inaccurate image of their abilities and consequently believe they can do more or less than is actually possible. Nevertheless, it can be an extremely valuable asset to administrators to critically assess their own abilities and behavior. They can then be in a better position to decide what to do about the gained insight.

There are times when people are led to believe they know more than they actually do. Assume that an administrator has an excellent understanding of the state drug and alcohol program. Should that administrator be recommended highly and be hired in a program in another state, the self-assessment ranking should drop because of the corresponding drop in some very important knowledge areas. However, the administrator may tend to rank himself/herself high by relying on past knowledge and the words of others. It may take some time before the high ranking could appropriately be earned by the administrator.

In any case, application of the self-assessment matrix should be a valuable guide to administrators. It can provide them with opportunities for turning knowledge into action, by systematically assessing their experience level with key administrative areas and their degree of familiarity with the systems of administration. Since administrative action tends to be quite varied and dependent on the circumstances in a given situation, attention will be directed toward the knowledge base in succeeding chapters.

Chapter 4

THE LEGAL ARENA

THE legal arena is very complex and impacts upon the organization and delivery of alcohol and drug services in more ways than most administrators realize. Yet, despite its comprehensiveness, not many programs have legal advisors to assist in reaching program decisions. This chapter is intended to provide administrators with an overview of the complex and perplexing nature of the legal arena and its actual or perceived impact on their decision-making behavior.

RELATING LAW TO ADMINISTRATION

Laws having a direct effect on the internal operation of an organization are quite naturally those which most easily draw the attention of administrators. These laws have greatest impact in the organization unit and organization unit-individual specific subsystems and may be divided into two areas: those which affect individuals in treatment and those affecting the nature of a program. In the former area fall laws pertaining to confidentiality, addict or patient rights, and affirmative action. Cognizance must also be given to the role of the defense attorney in regard to clients involved in court cases, in the diversionary process, or in seeking opportunities for successful rehabilitation. In the latter area are included laws pertaining to the development and operation of nonprofit and profit-making corporations, community-based facilities and related zoning, building, health, and fire codes, malpractice, contracts with other agencies, human consent forms for research, and the extent to which program counselors can offer clients paralegal advice.

Administrators must also keep abreast of legislation at the federal, state, and county government levels. Legislation is developed external to the treatment organization and would be

41

considered as part of the general and organization subsystems of administration. Such laws often serve to influence program philosophy and may indirectly or sometimes directly affect the treatment milieu. Laws which regulate the manufacture and dispensing of drugs, which classify some drugs as more dangerous than others, and which attempt to direct the thrust of any governmental effort, often reflect societal views and attitudes.

Input into the total legal arena seems to be a requisite for effective administration. Laws affecting clients and their treatment usually have a highly visible and direct impact inside an organization. Confidentiality regulations promulgated by the federal government are quickly read, interpreted, disseminated at staff meetings, and may appear as part of a policy manual. Treatment protocols, medical standards, and rehabilitative standards also tend to be similarly handled. In all such cases an administrator's response may be characterized as defensive because one is reacting to a predetermined situation.

Instead of reacting to an existing law, administrators may choose to help shape its development. They are in a very unique position and can do much to shape public and legislative views about the field, provided that they possess a high degree of credibility. They, too, must be willing to see the issues in the drug and alcohol field as probably related to one or more similar issues in one or more related fields. For example, laws on confidentiality must be viewed in the context of the general issue of confidentiality in law, as well as such other fields as medicine, counseling, and psychiatry.

Administrators can have an effect on the development of legislation. Although it may not be possible to individually shape or alter the outcome of a public law, one must keep in mind that laws are broadly written. Federal legislation must address the concerns of states, and state legislation must address the concerns of its counties or legislative districts, and so on down the legislative ladder. Sometimes local legislation may be enacted reflecting local concern that can serve to either support, increase, or decrease the intent of federal or state legislation. In these instances, contact with local public officials and key community people may indeed influence the outcome of local legislation.

In the context of social system decision making, an administrator needs to be aware of federal legislation and national attitudes affecting their development, while directing major efforts toward the development of local or state legislation, which usually has the most direct effect on program operations. This approach includes situations when local laws become a hindrance, and a state and federal focus is seen as a way of managing the situations. It recognizes that in the development of all legislation, the concerns of many constituencies usually alter bills introduced into legislatures. After enactment, one can usually expect a state or local response which administrators cannot overlook.

The wording of a public law is not the only consideration of administrators. Implicit in the previous paragraphs is the knowledge of administrators in understanding the process of public law enactment on all governmental levels and where one can intervene to be most effective. It is imperative for administrators to recognize where they can have optimum impact so that they can maximize their energies. It does little good to complain to a United States senator about state problems when talking to state senators might be more appropriate.

One area of the legal system is often overlooked. The implementation of public law is a determinant of administrative regulation. Quite often legislative change may not be necessary. Modifying program regulations may be more appropriate and practical. Considerable administrative interest, for example, should be directed toward the *Federal Register* and the various state registers, where public law is translated into administrative regulations governing programs and organizations.

For example, United States Congress Public Law 91-513, or the *Comprehensive Drug Abuse Prevention and Control Act of 1970*, authorized $29 million to be spent for drug abuse education over a three year period. It did not concern itself with how drug abuse education would be conducted, how programs would bid for funds, the criteria for fund awards, and other important areas of interest for program managers. These regulations always appear in the *Federal Register.*

Administrators, therefore, could have three arenas to focus their energies in relation to the legal system. The first is in the actual wording of legislation, another is in knowledge of the process of public law enactment at all governmental levels, and the third is in the development of administrative regulations governing the implementation of enacted legislation. Effective administration could be interpreted as the ability to appropriately guide the delivery of care according to legal constraints, devising a program treatment format which maximizes the flexibility of the constraints, and attempting to influence the development of more responsive law to the needs of the clients and program operations.

A key part to effective administration is credibility. One must recognize constantly that the highly volatile drug and alcohol field often creates credibility gaps in which virtually every official statement is suspect. Administrators do not need to bring further damage to their credibility by making public statements which do not reflect their knowledge of the problem, an understanding of past responses to the presenting problem or similar problems, their awareness of the public and political context of their program, and the difficulties that lie ahead.

Administrators should keep in mind that law is made by man and not preordained. By a single legislative act people can either become criminals or not be subject to prosecution. In 1973, Oregon became the first state to abolish criminal penalties for possession of one ounce of marijuana or less and replaced them with a maximum fine of $100. California and New York were the forerunners among state and federal governments in providing a civil commitment treatment procedure for narcotic addicts. Yet in 1977, the State of Tennessee Correction Commissioner, C. Murray Henderson, blamed marijuana laws for overcrowding that state's prisons. He estimated that up to 15 percent of the nearly 5,500 persons serving time in state prisons were there because of a marijuana or marijuana-related charge.[1] Crime reports from the FBI, which appeared in many

---

[1]Associated Press: Marijuana laws blamed in prison overcrowding. *Memphis Press-Scimitar, 97th Year,* February 24, 1977.

newspapers, showed that 445,000 arrests for marijuana were made in 1974, up 6 percent from 1973, and represented 69.4 percent of all drug arrests in 1974.

In addition to the legal picture and the varying public views regarding decriminalization of marijuana, there are likewise conflicting opinions regarding the use and possession of other drugs and alcohol. But while it is virtually impossible to clarify the many public views and conflicting opinions, other than to be impressed by the clarity of the many contradictions, there is also as much variation in the enforcement of existing law. Entrance into the criminal justice system is a primary function of arresting officers, and it is known that, depending on certain conditions, many people never enter the system.

The abundance of laws, rules, and regulations in the drug and alcohol field has not served to clarify much. On the contrary, these laws when taken together reflect a situation one might at best call vague and indecisive. A review and analysis of this situation in regard to several issues ought to provide administrators with sufficient cause to be extremely cautious when legal content is included in implementing their job responsibilities, particularly in talking with people in treatment or making public statements.

CATEGORIZING AND CONTROLLING ALCOHOL AND DRUGS

One set of laws serves to categorize and control drugs. In this century these laws have always kept alcohol separate and distinct from all other drugs. Although the history of American legal responses to alcohol and other drug use has been well documented on many occasions,[2] it is extremely important to note that prior to 1906, there had been no legal or legislative response to opiate addiction and alcohol intake. Indeed, nineteenth century America has been called a dope fiend's paradise.[3]

The passage of the first Pure Food and Drug Act of 1906

[2]*See*, for example, Brecher, Edward M. and the Editors of *Consumer Reports: Licit and Illicit Drugs*. Boston, Little, 1972, pp. 1-134; and Susman, Ralph M. Drug abuse, Congress and the fact-finding process. *Annals, AAPSS, 417*:16-26, 1975.
[3]Brecher, *Licit and Illicit Drugs*, p. 3.

brought America's first attempt to control opiate addiction. This was done by requiring medicines containing opiates and certain other drugs to so indicate on their labels. When the United States Congress passed the Harrison Narcotic Act in 1914, which cut off completely the supply of legal opiates to addicts, it also paved the way for the development of black-market narcotics.

As we approach the end of America's twentieth century, black-market narcotics continue to flourish. The legal picture from 1914 up to 1970, when Public Law 91-513 was enacted on October 27th of that year, became succeedingly complex and confusing. Public Law 91-513, or the *Comprehensive Drug Abuse Prevention and Control Act of 1970,* was designed to deal "in a comprehensive fashion with the growing menace of drug abuse in the United States, (1) through providing authority for increased efforts in drug abuse prevention and rehabilitation of users, (2) through providing more effective means for law enforcement aspects of drug abuse prevention and control, and (3) by providing for an overall balanced scheme of criminal penalties for offenses involving drugs."[4]

Part 1 of the same report by the Committee on Interstate and Foreign Commerce, House of Representatives, provided the clearest statement as to the necessity of the bill:

> Since 1914 the Congress has enacted more than 50 pieces of legislation relating to control and diversion, from legitimate channels, of those drugs referred to as narcotics and dangerous drugs. This plethora of legislation has necessarily given rise to a confusing and often duplicative approach to control of the legislative industry and to enforcement against the illicit drug traffic. *This bill collects and conforms these diverse laws in one piece of legislation based upon new scientific information, the restructured Federal law enforcement effort under Reorganization Plan No. 1 of 1968,* and greater information concerning the scope of the problem[5] [emphasis added].

---

[4]U.S. Congress, House, Committee on Interstate and Foreign Commerce, 91st Congress, 2nd Session, 1970, House Report 91-1444, p. 1.
[5]U.S. Congress, House Report 91-1444, p. 6.

Thus one point of origin had to do with an attempt to provide a uniform legislative code in this particular field. Another point of origin had to do with our international obligations under the Single Convention of 1961. Enactment of the bill would allow the United States "to immediately control under the schedules of the bill drugs hereafter included under schedules of the Single Convention upon the recommendations of the World Health Organization."[6]

America's legal response to alcoholism is well known. The Eighteenth or Prohibition Amendment passed both houses of Congress in December, 1917, was ratified by the required three-fourths of the forty-eight state legislatures by January, 1919, and went into effect in 1920. Prohibition lasted for thirteen years, when, in 1933, it was repealed by the Twenty-first Amendment.

During this thirteen year period it became painfully clear that Prohibition did not work. Alcohol was still available, enforcement problems arose and became unworkable, and the public witnessed an eruptive rise in black-market operations. The speakeasy replaced the saloon, and homemade alcohol replaced state and federally controlled manufactured alcohol.

Since 1933, there has been no sincere public or private legal attempt to control the manufacture of alcohol. The devastating and pragmatic effects of dealing with Prohibition have apparently cured all officials of the effort to control this drug.

Despite a plethora of scientific information revealing that alcohol is probably the most harmful drug of all the opiates and other narcotics to the mind and body, America has chosen to focus its legislative concern on the opiates. The effort has been complicated by the extensive use of certain addicting drugs such as amphetamines and barbiturates for medicinal purposes. The overall problem of control of opiate and narcotic drugs was thus made more difficult by the medical community when it began to qualify certain narcotic drugs as more beneficial than others. No longer was one talking about opiates and

---

[6]U.S. Congress, House Report 91-1444, p. 6.

narcotics as a class, but rather about specific restrictions, controls, and penalties for certain drugs.

The 1972-73 Fellows of the Drug Abuse Council observed that "the drug problem in America has often been simplified by its portrayal as essentially a *heroin* problem. Although there have been numerous statements and documented evidence on the dangers of other substances . . . the general thrust of public policies has been directed toward altering the consequences of heroin addiction."[7] In other words, only some drugs have been identified by public attention, while other more serious substances continue to go untouched.

In summation, our legislative response to the control of drugs may be charitably characterized as chaotic. As a nation we have simply not been able to control and regulate the growth of alcohol and drugs in our population. We have been able to control and regulate the manufacture of quality alcohol but have done nothing to limit how much can be manufactured. Yet certain narcotics are quality-controlled, and limitations are placed on how many can be manufactured. While some narcotics are deemed illegal to manufacture or to manufacture them in great numbers, we do possess a federal and state system of standards and quality control for legally manufactured alcohol and drugs. We can control and regulate the quality of the product, but not its growth. Alcohol therefore operates on the market principle of supply and demand, while the demand for amphetamines or barbiturates use is determined principally by the medical community. Drug manufacturers are supposed to produce drugs at a level congruent with the needs of the medical community. One should not underestimate the major efforts made and the pressure applied to convince physicians to prescribe more amphetamines or barbiturates for their patients.

Having had poor success with controlling the growth of drugs and alcohol through the manufacturing process, it seemed only logical that major emphasis for control would be on the people who use or abuse any of these drugs. For ex-

---

[7]Fellows of the Drug Abuse Council: Disabusing drug abuse. *Social Policy*, 4:43-45, 1974.

ample, the total of alcohol and alcohol-related arrests has already reached 55 percent of all arrests in the United States. Consider that "in 1965, out of close to five million arrests for all offenses, over 1,535,000 were for public drunkenness (31 percent), . . . over 250,000 arrests for driving while intoxicated, . . . [and] another 490,000 individuals were charged with disorderly conduct, which some communities use in lieu of the public drunkenness charge."[8]

A policy message in all these arrests seems clear: Since we as a nation cannot effectively ban alcohol and drugs from public consumption, we, as a nation, will tolerate public use of some but not all of them, and not in too much quantity; we will define those drugs the public may use and determine what quantity is to be considered as excess; we may also change the legitimacy and classification of those drugs from time to time and alter any penalties that go with these drugs; and furthermore, since one cannot achieve legal clarity on a national level, control of individual usage is viewed as a state or local matter. In such a situation chaos clearly emerges the victor and people in treatment the victims.

THE FOCUS OF THE DRUG AND ALCOHOL FIELD

The focus of the drug and alcohol system is a cause for considerable debate and a source of much consternation to administrators. The trouble is that, while the problem seems clearer than those problems arising from laws directed at the manufacture and control of all drugs, one is placed in the middle of a dilemma. The dilemma of whether alcohol and other drug abuse is to be viewed as a crime or as an illness is perhaps best illustrated by citing the legislative history of the *Comprehensive Drug Abuse Prevention and Control Act of 1970.* In this legislative action, Congress demonstrated its growing awareness of the rehabilitative approach to the problem of drug abuse. The underlying philosophy involved in the narcotics and drug abuse field seems to have been developed

---

[8]Brecher, *Licit and Illicit Drugs*, p. 261.

by the Prettyman Commission in 1963, which is cited specifically throughout House Report 91-1444. In effect, the Prettyman Commission recognized that the abuse of drugs had aroused two extreme attitudes, the punitive and the permissive.[9] The Commission did not accept either of these extreme attitudes, but it subscribed to certain aspects of each. The key point is that in 1963 the government began to consciously introduce the concept and practice of rehabilitation in the narcotic and drug abuse area.

Prior to 1970 Congress had enacted several pieces of legislation in the rehabilitation field for the 91st Congress to build upon. In 1963, Congress enacted the Community Mental Health Centers Act, authorizing federal matching grants for the construction of community mental health centers, among other things. In 1965 this legislation was amended to authorize federal grants to pay a portion of the costs of staffing these facilities. In 1968, this legislation was further amended to authorize specially marked funds for the construction and staffing of facilities affiliated with community mental health centers for the treatment of alcoholics or narcotic addicts.

Also, in the area of narcotic addict rehabilitation, the United States Congress enacted the Narcotic Addict Rehabilitation Act of 1966, which provided for increased federal efforts in the rehabilitation of narcotic addicts primarily through civil commitment procedures and increased efforts at rehabilitation. It did not elaborate on what those increased efforts would be in practice.

The central issue in Congressional debates on Public Law 91-513 was the pervasive conflict between the law enforcement and rehabilitative approaches to the narcotic and drug abuse problem. For example, the Committee on Ways and Means, House of Representatives, on August 12, 1970, stated:

> Legislation providing increased law enforcement authority in the field of drug abuse was transmitted to the Congress by the President on July 14, 1969. Because the proposed legislation

---

[9]Prettyman, Judge (Chairman): *U.S. President's Advisory Commission on Narcotic and Drug Abuse Report*, Washington, D.C.: U.S. Government Printing Office, 1963.

repeals the tax laws and other laws under the jurisdiction of the Committee on Ways and Means used to control narcotic drugs, the President's message was at first referred to the Committee on Ways and Means. However, because the proposed legislation also deals with drugs regulated under the Federal Food, Drug, and Cosmetic Act, the proposed legislation was divided into two bills, H. R. 13742 (referred to the Committee on Ways and Means) and H. R. 13743 (referred to the Committee on Interstate and Foreign Commerce). The two bills were, in general, identical, except with respect to the drugs covered by their provisions . . .[10]

Thus, one begins to see where the proposed legislation became split into several parts. Once the proposed legislation or H. R. 13743 was referred to the Committee on Interstate and Foreign Commerce, it was expanded to include the rehabilitative aspect of the drug abuse problem. The legislation had been considered in executive sessions before this committee on eight occasions, and Titles I (Rehabilitation) and II were ordered reported to the House unanimously on August 14, 1970 and together with Title III incorporated in the bill pursuant to action of the Ways and Means Committee.

The fact that the House had split the proposed legislation and referred it to two committees was extremely important. First, it allowed for the rehabilitative people to be heard, since the Committee on Interstate and Foreign Commerce also dealt with health issues. Second, it allowed for the health people to have a direct voice in the final compromises in the Act. Third, it allowed for an ease of passage through the House that did not occur in the Senate.

In the Senate, the proposed legislation was known as the Controlled Dangerous Substances Act, S. 3246, sponsored by Senators Dodd and Hruska. This bill was reported by the Judiciary Committee and was intended to reduce penalties for those convicted of using or possessing marijuana, among other things. It was basically a crime bill.

It was Senator Hughes who challenged and led the debate

---

[10]U.S. Congress, House Report 91-1444, p. 2.

over the jurisdiction of the Judiciary Committee when S. 3246 was proposed on the floor on January 23, 1970. He stated, "I believe . . . that before action is taken by the Senate on this legislation, it should be referred to its Committee on Labor and Public Welfare, pursuant to that Committee's jurisdiction over legislation relating to the public health. Such referral would have been entirely consistent with the traditional procedures of the committee system in the Senate when dual jurisdiction occurs."[11]

Senator Hughes kept this debate going the entire time S. 3246 was on the floor in January. He felt that input from the Committee on Labor and Public Welfare was necessary because "there are extensive provisions in this bill which relate not to law enforcement but to matters of public health."[12]

The Senator clarified his reason for insisting upon input from the Committee on Labor and Public Welfare, stating, "As I look further down this legislative path on which we are proceeding, when the bill goes to the House and the conference resulting, because of the procedures of this body, no members of the Committee on Labor and Public Welfare will be on the conference committee. They all will be from the Judiciary Committee, as the result of the assignment of the bill to that committee, unless the bill were referred to the Committee on Labor and Public Welfare."[13]

It should be clearly evident that only one major conflict arose during the time the various bills on drug abuse were discussed. This conflict was between law enforcement and rehabilitation and was mentioned specifically by several Congressmen. For example, Congressman Jarman stated, "As Members may recall, the scientific community and medical community of this Nation were greatly upset over the fact that scientific and medical decisions in the Senate bill were centered on the Department of Justice with the Attorney General having the responsibility to make scientific and medical determinations which were not in the competency of that Department, and

---

[11]Hughes, Senator: U.S. Congress, Senate, *Congressional Record, 116,* 91st Congress, 2nd Session, 1970, p. S482.
[12]Hughes, *Congressional Record,* p. S482.
[13]Hughes, *Congressional Record,* p. S487.

admittedly so."[14]

The concern stated by Congressman Jarman was, in part, what Senator Hughes had hoped to achieve in the Senate. However, the House members seemed much more responsive to striking a balance between the legal aspects and the medical aspects. Whereas the Senate pushed to keep these two aspects of drug abuse separate (at one point Senator Dodd indicated he would support Senator Hughes's drug abuse rehabilitation bill 1000 percent if he would let Senate bill 3246 pass without delay), the House merged these two concerns.

There was virtually no disagreement over the judicial components, Titles II and III, between the two legislative bodies. Indeed, Senate Bill 3246 formed the basis of Titles II and III of H. R. 18583 and was so noted in the Senate.

There was much discussion and controversy over the "no-knock" amendments to the bill. In the health arena there was much controversy over several key issues, including (1) limiting the attorney general's authority for conducting educational and research programs to those directly related to enforcement of the control provisions of the legislation, (2) giving greater authority to the secretary of HEW in the classification of controlled substances, and (3) providing for the confidentiality of information about patients or research subjects who have been promised anonymity by a government agency in exchange for highly personal information.

Senator Hughes had offered several amendments dealing with these three health issues in January, 1970, and all were defeated. However, in mid October, 1970, he indicated he was pleased that the amendments or the concepts behind them had become part of the legislation.

Another point which may have moved the Senate to include rehabilitation in the final bill was the fact that no legislation dealing only with law enforcement was going to pass the House. Indeed, the Senate realized that the House had registered a major plus by including the rehabilitation section.

The major Senate battle was centered on the jurisdictional dispute between the Judiciary and the Labor and Public Wel-

---

[14]Jarman, Representative: U.S. Congress, *House Congressional Record, 116,* 91st Congress, 2nd Session, 1970, p. H9112.

fare Committees. One outcome of this battle was the passing of the Hughes amendment on October 13, 1970, which surpassed the proposed Title I section of the House Bill. The Hughes substitute amendment for Title I of H. R. 18583 would have: (1) established a National Institute for the Prevention and Treatment of Drug Abuse and Drug Dependence within the Public Health Service of the Department of Health, Education and Welfare; (2) authorized a formula grant program and a project grant program to assist states and communities in planning, establishing, and carrying out a wide range of coordinated and comprehensive activities in the areas of drug education, prevention, treatment, and rehabilitation; (3) established an Intergovernmental Coordinating Council on Drug Abuse and Drug Dependence; (4) provided for the establishment of prevention, treatment, and rehabilitation programs for all federal civilian employees; and (5) incorporated the provisions in the House version of Title I which broadened the authority in the Public Health Service Act dealing with educational and research activities.[15]

The comprehensiveness of the Hughes amendment upset the legislative process. On one hand it was unacceptable to the House primarily because of its impact. On the other hand, Senator Hughes's effort and that of his associates is worthy of speculation.

Senator Hughes did have the opportunity to present a separate bill. When asked why no bill of this nature appeared before Congress, Senator Javits indicated that they had spent most of the time developing alcoholism legislation and could not get around to drafting drug abuse legislation. A more likely possibility is that passage of the Hughes substitute amendment would force a conference meeting between members of both Houses. This is the point where the Senate Labor and Public Welfare Committee would have major impact on the final legislation, which is what Senator Hughes had pushed for in January. The strategy appeared to be to force confrontation just prior to the final passage.

---

[15]Hughes, Senator: U.S. Congress, Senate, *Congressional Record*, 91st Congress, 2nd Session, 1970, p. S17395.

Throughout the development of Title I or the rehabilitation section of the Act and the many public hearings held on the subject, statistical evidence seemed helpful to Congress. For example, many senators in debate on the Senate floor referred to a National Institute of Mental Health survey of a student sample in a large university. The survey was reported by them to show that in 1967, 21 percent of these students had tried marijuana. The same students were sampled in 1968, and the results revealed that 57 percent had tried marijuana for an increase of 36 percent in one year. This survey apparently confirmed the necessity for reducing the penalties for the use and possession of marijuana.

Senator Hughes and his Special Subcommittee on Alcoholism and Narcotics had held hearings in 1969 and 1970. These hearings resulted in volumes of data and reports being produced regarding the state of our knowledge about alcohol and drug abuse. Much of the reported data and statements became redundant, but perhaps the wealth of information is best summarized and formulated in an approach by Doctor Roger Smith: "The goal should be to avoid criminalization to offer easy access to treatment facilities and make the opportunity to discontinue use readily available. If you fail to do this the therapeutic problems increase geometrically and you have a criminalized drug culture which tends to perpetuate itself which adds new recruits and makes treatment very, very difficult."[16]

Major opposition to the inclusion of Title I was voiced by the Nixon Administration. A memorandum was sent to the Senate in October, 1970, and read into the *Congressional Record* which clearly stated the Administration's reasons for excluding Title I. In their view, the legislation initially proposed was a judicial matter and they wished to keep it that way.

Opposition to the Administration's position came obviously from the medical and scientific community. Ample evidence of its impact on the legislators has already been given, which is the underlying theme throughout many of the statements cited

---

[16]U.S. Congress, Senate, Committee on Labor and Public Welfare, *Hearing Before the Special Subcommittee on Alcohol and Narcotics*, 91st Congress, 1st Session, 1969, p. 73.

in the Senate.

In general, H. R. 18583 went through the following process to enactment. In January, 1970, the Senate passed the Controlled Dangerous Substances Act (S. 3246). The House reviewed it and passed H. R. 18583 in late September, expanding the law enforcement focus to include a rehabilitative focus. In early October the House version was considered by the Senate, and it passed the comprehensive Hughes substitute amendment dealing with rehabilitation. The revised legislation went back to the House, which agreed to a conference report. The Senate did likewise, and a conference was held. On October 14th, both the House and Senate agreed to the conference report and forwarded it to the President for his signature. It was approved on October 27, 1970, and formalized the dual focus of drug and alcohol program efforts.

LAWS PERTAINING TO INDIVIDUALS

Much of the uncertainty and confusion plaguing the legal picture in the drug and alcohol field is reflected in laws pertaining to individuals. These laws include the positions taken by defense attorneys regarding their clients, confidentiality, the rights of addicts, and the right to equal opportunity or freedom from discrimination in all aspects of an individual's life.

One thread underlying these laws is the relationship between addiction and crime. This theme is obviously more important in relation to heroin use, in part because this drug seems symbolic of the whole field, while other drugs appear to be readily available or could be obtained easily or legally. Any black-market operation will serve to drive up prices, and this is precisely the case with heroin. In addition to its physiologic and psychological effects, heroin is a drug which society has outlawed and whose price is determined by its availability in the black market.

Society is a curious factor in the relationship between addiction and crime. While people clamor about heroin addicts, the fact is that society can create or eliminate people defined as criminals. For example, over 10 million people in the U.S.

could become criminals immediately, just by having the price of one ounce of alcohol to be equal to one ounce of heroin. The cost of one bottle of alcohol would be staggering, causing millions of alcoholics to steal to support their habit.

Nevertheless, the relationship between crime and addiction is a complicated and highly controversial public concern under constant investigation.[17] This concern has to do with the extent to which one holds addicts responsible for addiction-related behavior, i.e. do addicts commit criminal acts to support their *disease,* or are they criminals who also happen to be addicts? Fingarette believes "it is a grave mistake to try to meet the problem by declaring, falsely, that addicts have no control over their addiction-related behavior, and by declaring, on no good legal basis, that under the Constitution addicts as a class should not be subject to any penal sanctions for any addiction-related behavior."[18] This view suggests clearly that addicts are to be seen as criminals.

Greenberg and Adler have examined the relationship between crime and drug dependency according to the criminal history of the addict.[19] One of the three major areas explored in their study had to do with what they call the temporal sequence of criminal involvement. In this area they explored the question of an addict's criminal history prior to his or her habit.

The tentative conclusions of Greenberg and Adler on the temporal sequence issue make it clear that addicts cannot be treated as a class or as a totality. They reported on studies done by O'Donnell and Abrams in which both authors found that "those addicted prior to 1952 were predominantly non-criminal before onset of addiction, and for those addicted in 1952 or after, the relationship was reversed."[20] According to Greenberg

---

[17]Austin, Gregory A. and Lettieri, Dan J. (Eds.): *Drug Users and the Criminal Justice System.* Rockville, Md., NIDA, 1977; and Austin, Gregory A. and Lettieri, Dan J. (Eds.): *Drugs and Crime,* Rockville, Md., NIDA, 1976.

[18]Fingarette, Herbert: What is this affliction? *Center Magazine,* IX, 1976, p. 50.

[19]Greenberg, Stephanie W. and Adler, Freda: *Crime and Addiction: An Empirical Analysis of the Literature.* Harrisburg, Pa.: Governor's Council on Drug and Alcohol Abuse, n.d., Report No. 1.

[20]Greenberg and Adler, *Crime and Addiction,* p. 7.

and Adler, this change was due to the shift in populations sampled in early and more recent studies and to the passage of a series of stringent federal drug laws that were strongly enforced. For example, the Boggs Act, passed in 1951, which made first drug convictions carry a mandatory minimum sentence of two years and did not allow suspended sentences or probation on second offenses, resulted in a much higher cost for addiction to be maintained. The increases in cost and law enforcement brought about a sharp increase in the number of addicts, particularly black addicts, being sent to prison.

The Greenberg and Adler report is significant in that it empirically analyzes the relationship between crime and addiction between the years 1920 to 1973. Their general statements based on the literature seem to best summarize the crime and addiction issue at the present time. However, the following statements need to be considered in relation to the generally poor quality of research and the contradictions in the available data.

1. The majority of current heroin addicts have substantial criminal histories prior to the first use of opiates. Hence, the argument that addiction causes previously law-abiding persons to commit crimes is untenable.

2. Based on a single retrospective study of a normal population of black males, it would seem that while engaging in criminal acts does not lead to addiction in all cases, or even in most cases, it increases the probability of addiction.

3. Among addicts who are criminals prior to addiction, there is no reason to believe that addiction is the causal factor in increasing criminality. While crime may increase, it may have increased anyway, given the fact that most contemporary addicts are at an age which is also a high risk age for crime.

4. Contrary to early studies, the most recent evidence suggests that addicts commit primarily those crimes that yield a financial return, regardless of whether they are violent or not.[21]

However, the issue is far from settled. First, these general

---

[21]Greenberg and Adler, *Crime and Addiction*, p. 20.

statements pertain only to heroin addiction where one would naturally expect a high crime rate due to the present situation in obtaining the drug. Second, not all crime is committed by addicts. Their suggested probability that while engaging in criminal acts does not lead to addiction in all cases, it does increase the probability of addiction, may be more a consequence of the illegal character of heroin than to the drug itself. Indeed, it is generally conceded that nothing exists in the chemical makeup of heroin which causes people to commit crimes, but rather it is social policy issues and the defining of the drug as illegal which tends to make heroin users become criminals. Moreover, alcohol throughout the 1960s and early 1970s was by a wide margin this country's biggest law enforcement problem, with at least 40 percent of all arrests being made for drunkenness in a public place or being under the influence while driving.[22] In short, heroin users have had to bear the brunt of the country's apparent frustration at not effectively controlling substance use despite their not being the leading law enforcement problem in the United States. A change in the law could effectively change the nature of the relationship between crime and addiction.

The law was changed in practically all states when public drunkenness was decriminalized. This changed public policy by placing emphasis on detoxification programs and the availability of a continuum of care. In Minnesota, the legislature officially declared that "the interests of society are best served by providing persons who are dependent upon alcohol and/or drugs with a comprehensive range of rehabilitative and social services."[23] Since the twenty-six detoxification centers in Minnesota admitted 20,974 in the 1974 fiscal year,[24] one can easily see how many people were diverted from the criminal justice system.

---

[22]Brecher, *Licit and Illicit Drugs,* p. 261.
[23]Chemical Dependency Division, Bureau of Comprehensive Programs. *A Policy Change Toward Public Drunkenness, Minnesota's 3-Year Experience with Detoxification Programs.* St. Paul, Mn., Department of Public Welfare, 1975, p. 24.
[24]Chemical Dependency Division, *Policy Change,* p. 24.

Administrators need to strive for the best possible legal advice for their organization, their clients, and for themselves. Fullerton and Kurzman describe how defense attorneys have often provided no meaningful challenge to the testimony of the prosecution's analyst in marijuana cases.[25] As a result, clients have not been served well, as alleged illegal substances are often misidentified by chemists. When Kurzman applied his technique in the state of Minnesota, he found "state and city analytical chemists reluctant to testify in a case where they know they will be facing an attorney and scientist who are fully aware of the inadequacies of the common forensic tests for marijuana 'identification.' Accordingly, prosecutors are beginning to dismiss marijuana cases."[26] One can then witness the effects of expert legal advice on other people and in other systems.

ADMINISTRATIVE CONSIDERATIONS

While the legal arena does not appear to have the same impact on program operations than the other areas of administrative responsibility, it can often make the difference in one's degree of competence and understanding of administrative practice. Knowledge that society's attitudes in the drug and alcohol field of ambiguity and ambivalence are vividly reflected in its laws, one can better realize their effects on the formulation of social policy and the development of programming efforts. If people in programs are viewed by the public as being there because they recognize the need for treatment, one then finds it more acceptable to involve program clients in such things as determining their own course of treatment, involving them in program planning, and in perceiving them as having rights in the treatment process.

Administrators probably have greater familiarity with the laws pertaining to individuals, such as civil commitment procedures, confidentiality, and treatment consent forms, than with federal or state laws. However, they would be well advised

[25]Fullerton, Dwight S., and Kurzman, Marc G.: The identification and misidentification of marijuana. *Contemporary Drug Problems, III:*291-344, 1974.
[26]Fullerton and Kurzman, *Contemporary Drug Problems*, p. 331.

to become far more knowledgeable about federal and state legislation as they indicate trends and are often forerunners of actual program considerations. Moreover, they can provide opportunities for innovative organizational change, thereby casting one's organization in a highly favorable light.

Administrators should have access to employ or retain expert legal personnel. The complexities of law in general, the difference they can make in certain court cases, their advice in corporate and organization-related laws, and the interlocking of the health and criminal justice system in the diversionary aspect of the drug and alcohol field should be enough evidence for administrators to recognize when assistance would be needed.

Chapter 5

SOCIAL POLICY ISSUES

THE only real social policy issue is that no coherent and comprehensible national social policy exists in regard to drugs and alcohol use. Contradictions reign supreme, with laws suggesting one direction and actual practice dictating another, when economic or political considerations dictate an exception to regulations, or when policy guidelines are applied differently to substances, programs, and certain segments of the population.

In this chapter several contradictions in social policy will be explored. The outcome will not necessarily be clarity toward a national social policy, but rather a confirmation that one will probably never exist. People in drug and alcohol work should stop pursuing the national social policy illusion and learn to work with the uncertainty and degree of irrationality pervading the field.

DEFINING SOCIAL POLICY

Policy, in its simplest form, is a statement which reflects generally accepted definitions of interest or morality applicable to a significant number of people. It is intended to provide direction without dictating how to get there or what methods to employ. Policy informs all about what one would generally like to see happen, as expressed in goal statements.

Policy is articulated on all levels. It can be stated by people in the national limelight, by people at state and local seats of government, by boards of directors, and by administrators. Yet policy statements by administrators are viewed differently from those made by national leaders. Obviously, the more diverse and broad the audience of the policy statement, the more likely it is to be considered as public or social policy.[1]

---

[1]Gusfield, Joseph R.: The (f)utility of knowledge?: The relation of social science to public policy toward drugs. *Annals, AAPSS, 417*:4, 1975.

Public policy statements do not necessarily mean that they will be implemented. Statements made at the national level are usually contravened at other levels, when policy is placed in an action context. It is quite likely that in action situations other factors are considered before policy statements. For example, while there is much sentiment for encouraging people to enter treatment, once in treatment people face possible expulsion if they fail to adhere to agency rules and regulations.

In order to understand the substance of a policy, one must examine some related aspects of policy formulation. One such aspect is budget, which is discussed throughout this chapter. Allocation of funds show what the Government or an agency is actually doing, sometimes in contrast to what it is saying. Policy statements on any level are important only to the extent that they can be implemented and enforced. Decriminalization of marijuana remains a hollow federal policy effort despite numerous reports calling for significant changes in present policy.

FEDERAL RESPONSE TO DRUG AND ALCOHOL ABUSE

One of the major efforts of the decade 1965 to 1975 was the federal government's *war* on drug and alcohol abuse. In that decade, federal public policy was dramatically supported by huge outlays of funds for program development in health and law enforcement. The Special Action Office for Drug Abuse Prevention (SAODAP) was established in 1972 (Public Law 92-255), as a result of action by the Senate Subcommittee on Alcoholism and Narcotics. This office was to be an active participant in designing the federal drug abuse prevention budget and in formulating federal drug abuse policies. It was clearly a focal point of federal policy in drug and alcohol abuse for several years before it went out of existence. Presently the highest level coordinating authority for drug abuse activities in the federal government is in the Office of Management and Budget (OMB).

The same law which established SAODAP also required each

state to designate or establish a *single state agency* (SSA) if it wished to receive federal funds. The SSAs major function was to plan and coordinate that state's efforts in drug abuse prevention, which was broadly defined to include all nonlaw enforcement activities. The establishment of SSAs is significant in the federal response to drug and alcohol abuse, for it shifted drastically the relationship between the federal effort and federally funded programs at the city and county level. Basically, SSAs have brought about a change in federal budget allocation with more money directed toward drug abuse prevention programs, while also altering the impact of the federal policy effort.[2]

In the world of planning, the single state agency structure would have been a logical means of implementing federal policy goals while allowing states enough flexibility in their execution of these goals. The federal role would have been to clearly define policy goals and minimum requirements after appropriate input, and the state role would be to create the best programs and systems in each state in relation to federal goals. States would be implementors of federal policy and should not contradict federal policies. However, the SSAs have not functioned according to the perceptions of planners as described.

The major reason the SSAs have developed into articulators of state goals, which at times contradict federal policy goals, was due to a significant federal policy change in budget distribution. New Federalism was designed to increase the role of the states in management over the federal dollar. This policy change developed as part of a national political strategy by the Nixon Administration to secure more support for its own goals. Consequently, the states were allowed to allocate their formula grant money among the five funded categories according to their own priorities. Treatment and rehabilitation, education and prevention, training, and evaluation became subject to state priorities. Research was the only spending category in drug abuse prevention to remain a federal function with little state participation.

---

[2]Cline, Sibyl and Akins, Carl: *Governmental Response to Drug Abuse.* Washington, D.C., Drug Abuse Council, 1975, p. 3.

Coordination between agencies is another important factor to consider in federal policy formulation. Theoretically, coordination can make it possible for different organizations to work together and in support of national goals rather than working in support of their own organizational goals. Once again, practice sobers the theoretical view, and coordination between agencies is most problematic.

Akins and Cline describe how substance abuse as an operating policy concept is impeded in development on a federal level:

> The continued bureaucratic separation of the National Institute of Drug Abuse (NIDA) and the National Institute on Alcohol Abuse and Alcoholism (NIAAA) at the federal level, with the resulting frictions, lack of communication, and duplicative paper work, hinders the states in their efforts to plan and to improve service delivery. Those states whose agencies have the best coordination say that the greatest barriers to working even more closely together result from differences on the federal, not the state, level, and that the problems are more often with NIAAA than with NIDA.[3]

The national ambivalence regarding alcohol and drug abuse as a crime or as an illness is reflected in the generally poor degree of coordination with law enforcement efforts. On a national level law enforcement measures compete with health measures for the available dollar, and at a local level planning is thwarted by their differing purposes and orientation. Representatives of each field are likely to be at odds over which is the best way to handle the drug and alcohol problem. Further, federal funding for law enforcement efforts continues to be well endowed and out of the control of the SSAs.

Federal policy efforts have shifted to increasing state involvement and to decreasing federal impact on program development and operation with each state. Federal funds have been plentiful, although the rapid increases have leveled off in the past few years. States have the freedom to manage federal dollars according to their own priorities, except for research, but this policy action has not resulted in the promise suggested in

---

[3]Akins and Cline, *Governmental Response*, p. 24.

the law which established the SSAs. The articulation of a national drug and alcohol policy is also impaired by poor coordination between such organizations as NIDA, NIAAA, and law enforcement agencies and the separate federal funding of law enforcement measures. In this situation any federal policy statement can be expected to change as it is implemented. Further, one is not sure if federal policy is developed from a national interest or as a response to cumulative state interests.

Several authors are concerned about the development of social policy involving the combined factors of drugs, alcohol, legislation, and crime. The Fellows of the Drug Abuse Council "are convinced that the fixation on drugs and the consequent legal, medical, and sociopolitical abuses . . . are creating domestic problems far more monstrous than the original condition."[4] Fort asserts that crimes related to addiction, mainly crimes against property or prostitution in an attempt to buy fixes on the black market, are effects of our ineffective and misdirected drug control laws.[5] Murtagh, a former New York City judge, after years of case experience, concludes that the major reason drug treatment programs have not been very successful is because they all operate on the futile principle that an addict must be committed to be treated.[6] Legal punitive measures thus create more problems than they seek to solve.

Despite the accumulating evidence on the federal, state, and local levels about the incoherent nature of our drug and alcohol laws, the criminal approach still prevails. Treatment remains synonymous with getting the addict or the alcoholic out of the public's view. America flourishes as a drug-oriented society where drugs and alcohol have always been part of the daily dose of media programming. While society has generally accepted a chemical approach for solving unpleasant situations and difficult personal problems, certain drugs remain highly controlled by public policy. As long as society continues through legislation to favor certain drugs, also due to the eco-

---

[4]Fellows of the Drug Abuse Council: Disabusing drug abuse. *Social Policy, 4*:45, 1974.
[5]Fort, Joel: *The Pleasure Seekers: The Drug Crisis, Youth and Society.* Indianapolis, Bobbs, 1969.
[6]Murtagh, John M.: Criminal justice. In Straus, Nathan (Ed.): *Addicts and Drug Abusers: Current Approaches to the Problem*, 3rd ed. Boston, Twayne, 1971, pp. 62-71.

nomic impact of drug and alcohol usage on this nation's economy,[7] coherency and consistency in social policy is unattainable.

Moreover, public policy can be conflictual. While America's tobacco farmers, alcohol producers, and drug manufacturers continue to be supported by various government subsidies, the government also launches programs designed to prevent drug and alcohol use. For example, alcohol is now about a $20 billion business, and it advertises in order to sell its product. If the alcohol industry did not sell its alcohol, it would have a negative impact on the American economy. The result would probably bring government intervention designed to boost the ailing industry. Alcohol producers must have consumers. It is in their best economic interest if per capita consumption increases. Yet such an increase would result in greater alcohol abuse and greater problems in law enforcement, which may create more treatment and criminal justice programs. Social policy seems directed toward regulating personal morality (one can drink a lot but not so much as to become overly drunk). Social policy is becoming synonymous with social control, which may be the connection to the fundamental man versus state issue underpinning American society. If social policy becomes social control, then all must be willing to bear the consequences, and far too many drug and alcohol workers will have contributed without fully realizing their role.

STATE RESPONSE TO DRUG AND ALCOHOL ABUSE

State response has been established as a result of the Drug Abuse Office and Treatment Act of 1972. Much of the rationale and impact of the SSAs has been presented in the previous section, but it remains to discuss how the SSAs have operated within each state.

It should be noted that the creation of the SSAs occurred several years after the federal government had established an extensive treatment and rehabilitation thrust. Program people

---

[7]Mushkin, Selma: Politics and economics of government response to drug abuse. *Annals, AAPSS, 417*:27-40, 1975.

then developed an extensive network of personal contacts which bypassed state personnel. SSA development was viewed initially by program people with much skepticism and negativism, for it further removed them from direct contact with federal sources. Most SSAs therefore started out under difficult political circumstances.

Since 1972, SSAs have developed into formidable coordinating organizations. Most are now responsible for submitting annual drug abuse budgets to their state legislatures and for reviewing proposals for federal funds. State advisory councils to the SSAs have increasingly been the same people to review both the drug and the alcohol programs.

The SSAs have generally exerted their authority over program structure and service delivery in the treatment and rehabilitation programs. In most instances this is the system that had already been developed with federal funds, and assistance in developing program structures and improving service delivery systems was needed. The priority had already been established, and the SSAs responded to the inherited situation. This was the case in large states and in the Northeast. The middle and small sized states were heavily dependent on federal funds to support their treatment and rehabilitation programs.[8]

Methadone treatment programs reflected the SSAs intervention. State-operated methadone programs were growing rapidly, serving over 17,000 patients by the fall of 1972. Program operations were devised often as a response to federal regulations promulgated by the federal Food and Drug Administration (FDA) and the state regulatory agency. SSAs added a new source of regulations for program administrators to confront in managing their programs. Power struggles ensued between the SSA and the state regulatory agency for control over the methadone treatment programs, which were eventually won by the SSA. But during that time program administrators had to respond to at least those three regulatory agencies — not an easy task.

There are times when program administrators had different

[8]Goldberg, Peter, Sessler, John, and Schulte, Nancy: *Survey of State Drug Abuse Activities: 1972.* Washington, D.C., Drug Abuse Council, 1973, pp. 5-7.

regulations to meet in planning programs. One state devised a more stringent standard for counseling than the federal standard which, in order to meet it, would have resulted in a large increase of counseling staff. It was not clear who would fund such an increase. Upon inquiry it was learned that counseling hours per client could include a wide range of program activities in addition to actual counseling.

As SSAs matured they assumed more control over all drug and alcohol programs in each state. Federal program policy shifted accordingly, and the federal government began to contract with individual SSAs for program service delivery. State priorities shifted toward funding drug abuse prevention programs as well as treatment and rehabilitation programs. The shift was a means for state legislatures to take advantage of funds made available by the Federal Drug Abuse Education Act of 1970 and to redistribute the heavily concentrated treatment and rehabilitation funds throughout the state and into other program sources. The new arrangement made sense on a state level, but it certainly did not agree completely with federal policy statements at that time.

Single state agencies took advantage of federal technical assistance made available to them as part of the Drug Abuse Office and Treatment Act of 1972. The Drug Abuse Council reported on a needs survey taken by SAODAP that thirty-six out of forty-one states listed some areas of need. The most requested form of technical assistance was in developing the state master plan, followed in order by surveying the incidence and prevalence of drug abuse, establishing programs to assist business and industry, developing and operating a uniform data system, evaluating school and community education and prevention programs, evaluating treatment and rehabilitation programs, developing and establishing a licensing system, developing and operating training programs, and seventeen more areas of need.[9] The same report notes that "4 of the 6 areas of technical assistance most frequently requested are also necessary preconditions for receiving state formula grants under section 409 of the Drug Abuse Office and Treatment Act of

[9]Goldberg et al., *Survey of State Drug Abuse Activities,* p. 17.

1972.''[10] Thus did SAODAP insure that SSAs would address the management function of planning and evaluation, precisely the areas most lacking in federally funded treatment and rehabilitation drug abuse programs.

Most SSAs now also function as the financial base for state drug and alcohol programs. They receive their funds from federal sources and state legislatures and allocate those funds according to the priorities established in the state drug and alcohol plan. More SSAs are being merged into one operation with substantial benefits in reducing administrative costs, increasing expertise, increasing public awareness, and in local program efforts. Merger does not occur without much travail, as one might expect, due to the various lobbies in state legislatures.

It is obvious that states vary in SSA development. States with strong SSAs have assumed a more powerful role in shaping state policy and influencing federal policy. The establishment of programs to assist business and industry is an excellent example of policy formulation on a state level, which has apparently had broader implications. Presently, it appears as if social policy has its greatest impact at the level of state government rather than at the level of federal government.

LOCAL RESPONSE TO DRUG AND ALCOHOL ABUSE

The local response was different from the federal or state policies on drug/alcohol abuse. There was no legislative mandate establishing a special office, so interested cities and counties usually assigned a coordinator or liaison person to work with and monitor local programs. The coordinator could have been an employee of the city or county mental health and mental retardation program, or some other similar agency, or operating as staff of the chief county executive office.

A coordinator generally assumed overall responsibility for coordinating or directing the community's response to the drug and alcohol problem. Greatest success was with treatment and rehabilitation programs, as coordinators had virtually no juris-

---

[10]Goldberg, et al., *Survey of State Drug Abuse Activities,* p. 18.

diction over the local law enforcement program or over the public education system's drug program. When the Drug Abuse Council surveyed city and county drug abuse activities in 1972, they found that "whenever a municipally sponsored drug treatment and rehabilitation program did exist in the local jurisdiction, 51 percent of the city coordinating agencies and 42 percent of the county coordinating agencies had budgetary control."[11]

Cities and counties continue to rely on state government for financial aid to operate their drug and alcohol programs. States had always financially supported these programs, and with the creation of the SSAs and the increased amount of local match funds for federal grants renewals, the dependence on state government became even greater. Federally funded projects looked to the state for funds to continue their operation and were forced to compete with other drug and alcohol related programs for available funds.

The increased dependence on state funds has also resulted in an increase in policy control by the state. Local programs applying for renewal grants or contracts had to comply with SSA-developed criteria for funding, particularly in states where the SSA was strong. State policy became important, and such policies as citizen involvement in planning and coordinating local responses were implemented. Another reason for this increase in state policy control could be seen in the federal budget, which in fiscal year 1975 increased drug abuse prevention funds and decreased treatment and rehabilitation funds. State agencies strongly supported the former, and in order to compete for dwindling dollars, the treatment and rehabilitation programs were increasingly compelled to turn to the state for continued operations.

Local operations provide an excellent opportunity to examine their relationship to state and federal policy statements. Rehabilitation of the heroin addict was an often stated goal of methadone maintenance programs. Employment of methadone maintenance patients was considered an essential ingredient in

---

[11]Goldberg, Peter, Sessler, John, Danielson, Deborah Marks, and Johnson, Jean: *Survey of City/County Drug Abuse Activities: 1972.* Washington, D.C., Drug Abuse Council, 1973, p. 21.

their rehabilitation process. Despite many efforts, the unemployment rate among former heroin addicts has remained high, primarily due to the attitudes of private employers. Rehabilitation remains largely a goal.

Law enforcement activity continues to be well supported financially. Since 1965, cities in the 50,000 to 250,000 population range have reported the largest increase in the establishment of special narcotic units, followed by counties in the 100,000 to 250,000 population range. Many large cities and counties, each holding over 250,000 people, had already established special narcotic units within their police forces.[12] At the end of 1972, jurisdictions reporting law enforcement information on their special narcotics units spent in excess of $26 million annually on drug law enforcement efforts.[13] Thus, law enforcement was as predominant a goal as was treatment in drug abuse policy.

IMPACT ON ADMINISTRATION

It is quite apparent that policy changes have affected program operations. These policy changes have happened external to the facility or the program and apply to the general and organizational subsystems of administration. It was noted that administrators in these two subsystems have least control, and the shift in federal policy to fund drug and alcohol programs through single state agencies emphasizes the point. Indeed, the shift was already occurring in intergovernmental relations, and some administrators were better able to detect the trend by developing statewide relationships.

Administrators are understandably prone to overlook the impact of federal or state policies. Gusfield notes that "in the world of daily existence there is much more ambivalence, ambiguity and contradiction than the generalized rules and formulations of public policy can admit . . . Rules are formulated in general terms, but they are applied in specific solutions."[14]

---

[12]Goldberg et al., *Survey of City/County Drug Abuse Activities*, p. 17.
[13]Goldberg, et al., *Survey of City/County Drug Abuse Activities*, p. 17.
[14]Gusfield, *Annals, AAPSS*, p. 14.

Since one has to confront problems on a daily basis, federal and state pronouncements tend to have little visible impact on the worker-client relationship. One cannot convince unemployed ex-addicts that rehabilitation is a major policy thrust in drug abuse program efforts. Goal statements cannot be offered as a way to solve practical problems.

Administrators must, however, keep pace with changing policies external to their organization, with survival being probably the best reason, as when shifts in funds occur. When treatment funds started to decline, administrators could have developed drug abuse prevention programs in order to maintain a certain level of funding. Expanding the base of program operations can be an excellent method for retaining a degree of influence in policy formulation. For example, as new programs are developed as a response to state priorities, old programs tend to lose some of their political clout. Opting to keep pace with the change enables one to remain current and, hence, not to lose any political clout.

Policy formulation within an agency is subject to the same problems as policy developed outside an agency. In other words, policy statements made on a board level may have little relationship to the worker-client relationship. Board people may subscribe to the rehabilitation policy but develop no coherent employment component inside the program. Such activity is not different from the discrepancies observed among federal, state, and local program policies. Consistency between board or local program policies and program operations is in the greater control of administrative action.

Legislation serves as a key source in policy formulation. Congressional action indicates where federal or state funds will be appropriated and eventually allocated. Administrators have to respond accordingly and, in the case of older programs, make room for the new services or program components. Publicly funded programs are obviously more prone to public policy changes. Privately funded programs have to respond more to clients' ability to pay. Legislation will therefore continue to more directly affect programs that depend on public financial support.

It is interesting to note the discrepancy between program operations and the more enlightened disease or illness concept of drug and alcohol abuse. While many programs have been funded according to the treatment and rehabilitation model, clients in publicly supported programs are there more as a response to the criminal justice system. Clients often enter drug programs as a result of court action or proposed legal action, as do some alcoholic clients when certain crimes are committed while intoxicated. The growing relationship between the criminal justice and the health systems should be cause for considerable concern over the motivation for program development. Client control achieved through health and medical measures is the same as client control through legal measures. At times, it may even be more difficult for clients in treatment to escape the diagnostic labels given to them by medical personnel. The issue seems to be able to clearly identify what one is treating — the client or society's desire to be free from drug and alcohol deviants.

Policy statements at any level are intended to apply equally to all people covered by them. In reality this does not happen all the time. Employment of former heroin addicts is complicated when private employers are asked to employ black people. Labor statistics verify that race is an important factor in employment practices, and when inflation and a poor economy are present, hiring is made even more difficult. Obviously, racial and cultural factors must be considered in policy formulation and policy implementation.

One must surely ponder the role of research and scientific information in policy development. The scientific community was instrumental in expanding the national thrust of drug abuse activities to include a rehabilitative focus when its representatives spoke at hearings prior to the passage of the Comprehensive Drug Abuse Act of 1970. Scientists have not been as successful in convincing the public about the relative dangers of all drugs, as alcohol and barbiturates, while being more dangerous to the body, are viewed with far greater tolerance by the public than is marijuana. The mitigating factor is, of course, public attitude and its view of *drugs* as illegal and harmful and *alcohol* as a social lubricant.

The preponderance of research is in the biomedical and treatment aspects of the drug and alcohol phenomenon. Researchers have spent much time and effort in studying the biochemical aspects of drugs, their chemical reaction in the body, the identification and explanation of various treatment modalities, in doing incidence and prevalence studies, in conducting follow-up studies, and so forth. Applied research to policy making has only been a recent concern, or starting with the advent of evaluation research. As more of this type of research is conducted, there will be apparent a greater input by researchers into policy decisions.

After almost a decade of increased public visibility and rapid increases in available public funds, it is expected that the public would begin to shift its attention to other social problems. By 1975, there was growing public sentiment that the drug problem had reached its peak of public concern. Budget shifts were made, legislative solutions had apparently been exhausted for the moment, and the public felt confident that it had created enough organized mechanisms to regain control over the situation. The drug and alcohol abuse problem has not abated, but public attention has waned. The public message appears to center on observing the outcomes of the funds made available to the newly created armada of drug and alcohol experts.

Chapter 6

PLANNING AND
FINANCIAL CONSIDERATIONS

PLANNING is the most abused aspect of administration. It is a requirement of every program at practically all levels of decision making and can consume much time and effort. Yet in proportion to the energy expended, planning does not produce the results its proponents espouse. In this context it is oversold as a panacea of organizational problems and social ills.

While many planning activities can be considered worthwhile, most people simply neglect the limitations of planning itself. Competent administration depends on appropriate insights from a number of sources both inside and outside the drug and alcohol program, and planning is but one of the sources. Appreciation of what planning can and cannot do would greatly enhance its receptivity in administration practice. The kinds of activities covered in this chapter are considered central to the development of the agency product and to which all programs would have appropriate staff.

In the drug and alcohol field the product is the outcome derived from a set of interactions between clients and workers. Thus, the nature of planning and its relation to the treatment process, the organization of services, fiscal management, interdisciplinary collaboration, and consultation are seen as integral to the development and implementation of drug and alcohol programs. While research and evaluation does contribute to the shaping of programs, it is discussed separately in Chapter 7 because of its complexity and lack of a uniform program staffing requirement.

There are some important distinctions to be clarified in regard to planning from an administrative perspective. Administration requires decisive action and a responsibility for such actions, whereas planning and planning-related activities are used as parts of the administrative process. A planner's role is therefore most typically that of an advisor to the more politically oriented administrator.

In an advisory capacity, planners usually perform a minimum of four basic services to administrators.[1] These services include (1) defining problems and issues, (2) collecting data about the identified problems and presenting the analysis, (3) presenting alternative solutions to the problems and recommendations for action, and (4) providing continual advice about the effects of plans. Planners have been increasingly used as ancillary personnel to administrators by working directly with client or consumer groups in implementing their services. They have also been used to train community people, staff, politicians, and other participants in the various parts of the planning process. Thus, planners advise administrators and administrators supervise planners.

A second distinction is the difference between a plan and a planning process. A plan is the written or otherwise visible end product of a series of related activities designed to systematically and thoughtfully solve problems and chart the course of future events. The planning process is the series of related activities which, when completed, culminate in a written document or plan. The planning process is therefore crucial for administrators to control, for it is dynamic, usually involves many participants, is conducted over a long period of time, and has the potential for producing organizational change.

The distinction between a plan and a planning process has another practical consideration. It would be extremely difficult to employ someone to *write a plan* because this activity cannot be accomplished without some sort of planning process taking place. This point must often be clarified with planners when discussing the extent of their involvement in program development. Administrators can negotiate for and clarify the planning model used in plan development.

A third distinction is in the nature of work. All planners start

---

[1]Catanese, Anthony James: *Planners and Local Politics: Impossible Dreams.* Beverly Hills, Ca., Sage, 1974, p. 44.

from the end phase and work backwards in time. For example, a planner would first identify the final submission data and plan specific activities in relation to that date. Each activity in the planning process is connected directly to a time frame, so that determining objectives might take three days or writing the first draft about seven days. Administrative work ordinarily does not proceed in this manner, so the two types of personnel often work under different conditions and time constraints.

The complexity of planning and related problems tends to vary according to the subsystem in which it occurs. Inside a drug and alcohol program, one is very likely to view planning entirely in the context of securing a grant or a contract. There is very little real long-term planning done on an agency level in the drug and alcohol field. The greatest amount of planning occurs when a new service is being secured or when meeting continuing grant or contract requirements. On a state or national level, planning can proceed with theoretical and abstract guidelines. For example, service integration and continuity of care are theoretically sound planning constructs from a state or national planning perspective, but tend to be highly idealized when applied on a program level. It is one thing to logically show how service integration between the drug and alcohol programs and existing community services such as employment, vocational rehabilitation, and education would take place, but this effort has not demonstrated any significant benefit to clients. The interests of planners are more in producing complete plans than in struggling with the difficult tasks of delivering services to clients. After all, these are the very same service agencies which have not been very responsive in the past to the problems of drug and alcohol clients.

The differing interests between federal and state planners and program planners is a constant source of irritation for administrators. Program planners realize it is often impossible to actually implement the grand schemes envisioned by federal and state planners. Continuity of care may be possible to achieve on a broad scale by showing that clients have a range of services available to them in a community when all programs are considered. However, broad scale planners rarely consider client difficulties in obtaining needed services, so that the recognition of continuity of care on a local level is rarely addressed. It is much easier to write in a plan that continuity of care exists rather than to achieve it in actual practice. This deviance has, at times, been interpreted negatively when federal and state people evaluate administrative performance. It seems that they and the society they represent tend to be the real sources of the problem.

The issue is not that continuity of care and service integration are not worthwhile program objectives, but rather that their attainment in drug and alcohol programming is beyond the control of administrators. Broad scale planners have a marked proclivity for holding administrators accountable for implementing continuity of care, service integration, and other planning concepts important to them without as much consideration whether the concepts make any difference from a client's perspective or from a program management level. Federal and state planners and evaluators simply hold administrators accountable; they do not become involved in the organizational clashes, political realities, and effects on the client population which really determine the direction of the drug and alcohol field. Matlins probably best summarizes this problem of form over substance in planning:

> All too often, the planning activities that have taken place to help allocate resources in the drug field have been characterized by their separation from the reality of the world, as well as the reality of the organization intended to carry out the plan. Federally mandated requirements to plan are laudable in intent and frequently laughable in result. The planning activity is often seen as an erroneous chore that must be carried out in order to receive federal funds . . . In such a system, the planning process has been used primarily to produce the 'paper plans' needed to satisfy federal requirements and get the funds distributed within the state, rather than to identify need, establish priorities among competing objectives, and allocate resources systematically.[2]

---

[2]Matlins, Stuart M.: Planning: a personal view and some practical considerations. *Annals, AAPSS, 417*:47, 1975.

THE PLANNING PROCESS

The planning process can afford administrators with an excellent opportunity for staff involvement and participation in program operations. In many instances deadlines for grant or contract submissions are known well in advance, and this time can be used constructively. All too often administrators let this valuable time slip away, are faced with an imminent deadline, and then take reactionary and elitist steps to write the required document. There are times when an immediate response is required, such as responding to a request for proposal (RFP) or applying for a special program, which does limit the extent of involvement by others. Staff understand and accept when such limitations are imposed on administrators, but view with skepticism when crisis planning becomes the norm.

One could design a planning process which would facilitate administrative practice. Catanese describes the seven basic steps in the planning process that he feels would be acceptable to most planners, which are as follows:

(1) The identification and definition of problems and their interrelationships.
(2) The determination of the community's objectives in dealing with each problem, as well as the totality of problems.
(3) An appraisal of the existing plans, programs, and decisions for dealing with the problems to determine if they are adequate.
(4) The formulation of alternative recommendations for solving the problems according to the community objectives.
(5) The evaluation of the alternatives by analyzing the predictable by-products and side effects, as well as the approximate costs and benefits.
(6) A recommendation for adoption of the most appropriate alternative by the decision-makers.
(7) The possible modification of the recommended alternative according to feedback from the community and elected officials.[3]

While planners might agree with this idealized model of the

---

[3]Catanese, *Planners and Local Politics*, pp. 44-45.

planning process, it is at this present time highly inappropriate in the drug and alcohol field. A somewhat more realistic planning process might proceed in the following manner. A problem is either identified by drug and alcohol personnel or it is identified for them by another source. The identified problem is then matched with the availability of funds, which also sheds light on its relative importance in each funding cycle. Having identified a problem and a potential source of funds, the application kit is obtained for review by program personnel. Assuming that one wants to proceed, a series of meetings would be held, most likely involving people from all staff levels in the organization and representatives of the board of directors or advisory board. These meetings would be designed to obtain the support of these people and the groups they represent as well as to discuss the actual development of the proposed program. Contact with the funding source would be made in order to obtain their input and response to the proposed program. Depending on the extent of the suggested changes in the proposed program, administrators would either return to the people involved in planning for their review and comment or complete the application themselves. In either case administrators would assume responsibility for insuring that the application is completed and submitted accordingly.

Administrators need to be more skillful in understanding an administrative planning process, such as the one just described, which more realistically reflects their activity. Teaching administrators about an idealized planning process is inappropriate simply because their needs are more attuned to the political actualities of obtaining funds for their programs and other similar tasks. Planning in the political context proceeds quite differently from planning in training sessions or in the classroom.

Planning quality programs does not have to proceed according to an idealized planning process. In planning programs administrators ought to use any technique and method which works best for them, although there are some very important principles to follow. First, all people who will be affected by the development, implementation, and monitoring of the proposed program must be kept informed throughout the entire planning effort. Second, there must be a clearly articulated and logical process which relates all participants to each other over the planning period. This action is necessary so that one can easily see what is required, know who is to do the work, and understand one's contribution to the total effort. Third, people must be notified as soon as possible if there are any changes and the reasons for the changes in the planning effort. This is done to minimize any notions of manipulation.

A fourth principle for planning programs would be to share with planning participants all information pertinent to the proposed program. Withholding certain information is destined to weaken the total effort and usually is the cause of serious problems later in the program.

Basically, administrators must develop an administrative planning process and follow the dictates of idealized planning process models. Administrative planning models would account for the nature of competition, the political context of the drug and alcohol field, the inclusion of funding sources, and the availability of funds. Such a model and its related principles is much more appropriate to the needs of administrators.

ORGANIZATION OF SERVICES

In the drug and alcohol field services are organized according to three categories. These categories are primary, secondary, and tertiary. It is possible to relate each service provided to clients to one of these categories.

Primary services are involved with preventing the onset of the illness. These services are usually the most difficult to assess for impact and perhaps the least likely to affect specific individuals. For example, drug and alcohol education programs aimed at the school and the community environments would be placed in this category. However, one must wait years before conclusively determining whether these programs had any effect on the exposed population in preventing drug and alcohol usage from being problematic.

Short-term methods for assessing the effects of primary prevention in schools can be useful for planning programs of this type. These methods compare the attitudes and behaviors of students exposed to primary services with nonexposed students. Community-efforts are much more difficult to assess, as they frequently require the conducting of an incidence and prevalence study to obtain needed information.

Primary services tend to be directed toward large numbers of people and not targeted to any specific individual. For example, drug and education programs would be directed toward groups of people by either age, sex, or interest. Thus, programs could involve seventh graders, girls or boys clubs, or debate or photography clubs. The effort is toward exposing many young people to the dangers of drug and alcohol use and abuse, for these tend to be the class of people at greatest risk.

The educational orientation of primary service programs may be a derivative of the problems identified in the legal arena. This emphasis places enormous responsibility on individual will, in the context of high pitched marketing and advertising thrusts by the multi-billion dollar drug and alcohol manufacturers. Such an imbalance provides for a weighted contest, and this country will always have drug and alcohol clients.

An alternative to the educational orientation would be to control the results of individual drug and alcohol abuse through harsh legal and police measures. For example, Japan has virtually eliminated drunk driving by instituting severe penalties for violators. Violations are placed on personnel records and result in little or no job advancement. Consequently, when people drink they leave their cars at home, use public transportation, or make other arrangements.

Secondary services include hot lines, rap groups, coffee houses, and those programs which serve to link people seeking treatment with other community services. The major activities in this category are intake, referral, assessment, and crisis intervention. Staff is usually trained to work intensively with people for short periods of time, particularly during crisis situations. The target population addressed generally is young, with varying degrees of drug and alcohol experimentation, who do not perceive themselves as having primarily a drug and alcohol problem.

Tertiary services are more commonly known and synonymous with treatment and include all other programs. Detoxification units, day-care centers, residential centers, methadone treatment centers, and group homes are some examples of the range of programs which are in this category. People in treatment are seen as having a major drug and alcohol problem, usually follow some form of a treatment regimen, require long-term care, and may have various medical problems from prolonged drug and alcohol abuse as well as a range of social problems.

Services in the tertiary services category are more individual-oriented. An individual's problem is defined in a medical context which necessitates the development of an individualized treatment plan. Clients are supposed to use the available individual and group activities in accordance with their treatment plan. The range of services available in each program minimally includes intake and referral and individual counseling and group counseling and would expand to offer drug therapy, family counseling, detoxification, inpatient treatment, medical care, vocational counseling, employment solicitation, court-related counseling, self-help groups, follow-up or aftercare, and various other services, depending on the specific nature of a program.

Programs in the drug and alcohol field treat groups of alcoholics and drug addicts separately. The literature is replete with program descriptions, evaluation studies, and other research which study either alcoholics or drug addicts. Combining these two populations in a merged treatment program is a recent development which could bring some change in how services are designed and operated.

Ciotola and Peterson compared selected personality characteristics of groups of alcoholics and drug addicts in a mixed inpatient treatment facility.[4] Their results indicated many similar personality characteristics and dynamics underlying drug abuse, and they did not see any insurmountable problems for

---

[4]Ciotola, Paul V. and Peterson, James F.: Personality characteristics of alcoholics and drug addicts in a merged treatment program. *Journal of Studies on Alcohol*, 37:1229-1235, 1976.

planning treatment efforts. Age is the most significant personality characteristic in mixing groups, with alcoholics being older.

Other research supports the movement toward merged program planning. Ottenberg and Rosen concluded that the advantages outweighed the disadvantages when they evaluated an Eagleville merged treatment program.[5] Also, Baker, Lorei, McKnight, and Duvall did not detect large differences in outcome measures when alcohol and drug abuse programs were combined and conventional treatment environments were compared at the six month point.[6] Their results also encourage retention of the traditional proven treatment modalities, particularly in the case of the alcohol-dependent client.

It is generally recognized that a highly significant number of people in treatment are polydrug users. It seems inevitable that this occurrence be given full recognition by the various funding sources, but as yet there is an incredibly small amount of literature on merged treatment programs. Further, no reliable data is available on the impact of these merged treatment programs in management. The Veterans Administration is moving toward single program management in the drug and alcohol field, and perhaps they will develop some research in this area.

THE ROLE OF ACCOUNTING

Many administrators lack basic knowledge and understanding of accounting. They are unable to study and interpret financial reports. Consequently, they are even less able to evaluate the results of past program operations with accuracy and to shape future policies with greater awareness. Knowledge of accounting can provide administrators with a rich source of support for everyday decisions. Better records would be kept, financial records would be more readily understood, and mone-

[5]Ottenberg, D. J. and Rosen, A.: Merging the treatment of drug addicts into an existing program for alcoholics. *Quarterly Journal of Studies on Alcohol, 32*:94-103, 1971.
[6]Baker, Stewart L., Lorei, Theodore, McKnight, Harry A. Jr., and Duvall, Jeffrey L.: The Veterans Administration's comparison study: alcoholism and drug abuse — combined and conventional treatment settings. *Alcoholism: Clinical and Experimental Research, 1*:285-291, 1977.

tary decisions would be made more intelligently.

It is generally agreed that accounting provides a record of business transactions in financial terms.[7] Systems are designed by accountants in order to obtain the necessary information for the record. Bookkeeping emphasizes technique, whereas accounting emphasizes the design of business records, data analysis, and the preparation and interpretation of reports based on the records. Bookkeepers enter business transactions in the record, which are actions involving an exchange of values such as purchases and sales of goods or services. Accounting records show the effects of the business transactions on the assets, liabilities, and equity of the legal status of the program. These effects are summarized on a regular basis in at least three major financial statements. The balance sheet provides a list of assets, liabilities, and capital of an organization as of a specific date; the income statement summarizes income and expenses of an organization for a specific time period (thirty, sixty, or ninety days); and the funds statement indicates funds obtained and their source in the accounting period covered by the report and their disposition.

The time has come for administrators to assume greater responsibility and authority in this area. The task of preparing and interpreting financial reports has generally been assumed by treasurers on boards or by accountants, with administrators nominally involved. Continued involvement by board representatives and accountants are advocated and crucial to effective management. However, administrators who understand the fiscal reports can make more appropriate program decisions and make better use of board people and accountants for advice and in determining policy.

While thorough understanding of the field of accounting is not possible in this text, additional pieces of information are needed to understand the fiscal records. The fundamental balance sheet equation is assets equals liabilities plus capital (Assets = liabilities + capital). It shows the balance between

[7]Bauer, Royal D. M. and Darby, Paul Holland: *Elementary Accounting.* New York, Barnes & Nobel, 1973. *See,* also, Gross, Malvern Jr.: Financial and Accounting Guide for Nonprofit Organizations. New York, Ronald, 1974.

assets (anything of value owned), *liabilities* (debts), and *capital* (the owner's equity or the excess of assets over liabilities). The equation shows the equality between property ownership, including rights in property, and the claims of owners and creditors against the property. There are two kinds of claims: those of outside creditors and those of the owner or owners. In all cases, creditors' claims rank ahead of the equity claims of the owners because they are contractual. Thus, should an organization go bankrupt, its creditors have preferential rights to the assets.

Most organizations use the accrual basis of accounting. This method provides a more accurate presentation of the financial statements because it includes such things as unpaid expenses or incoming funds from services rendered. This additional data is required if one is trying to obtain the cost of treatment or attempting to draw conclusions from the statements regarding the financial strength or weakness of a particular service.

In contrast, the cash basis of accounting reports transactions only when cash has been received or expended. One major advantage is its simplicity, and nonaccountants can easily understand the records. It usually requires the keeping of checkbook stubs and does not require extensive accounting experience. It is not used extensively because the cash basis in many instances does not accurately illustrate an organization's financial position. Gross points to the difficulty of nonprofit organizations in effectively using a budget as a control technique without being on an accrual basis. He notes, for example, that cash basis organizations have difficulty because payment may be delayed for a long time after incurring obligations.[8] This is precisely the situation when third-party insurance benefits are applied for and a sixty-to-ninety day reimbursement period is usual.

FISCAL MANAGEMENT

There is no doubt that every administrator in this field is

---

[8]Gross, *Financial and Accounting Guide*, p. 22.

well aware of the need for fiscal management. Indeed, the full impact of fiscal planning now being felt by administrators in other health and social welfare programs had its start in the early 1970s in the drug field. A matrix was required by federal representatives along with the continuing grant application. This matrix forced programs to arrive at a cost per treatment slot, obtained by dividing the number of people able to be treated at one time into the total number of dollars spent in a particular service area, such as inpatient or outpatient. A national norm was projected by federal sources and generally recognized in planning programs. Soon this fiscal procedure was extended into the alcohol field. Thus, fiscal management has been an integral planning consideration in the drug and alcohol field for many years.

Unfortunately, fiscal management has not been at the core of administrative competence. This task has usually been assigned to consultants or others appearing to have a greater understanding of the world of finance. Administrators have spent most of their effort in tending to the development of treatment modalities and learning the managerial tasks for experts or management consultants.

Fiscal management is the hub of administration. It is the relationship of program dollars to manpower and the number of clients served in the context of specified services, and it identifies the cost per client per service. Conventional budgeting techniques known to administrators, such as zero-based budgeting and cost-benefit analysis, accounting techniques, and policy directions, are incorporated in fiscal management.

Administrators need to be continually involved in all decisions pertaining to fiscal management. Budget preparation involves policy decisions, since funds are allocated as a result of this effort. It is wise to include others in budget preparation, such as a treasurer or key staff or board people, so that policy decisions can be made appropriately. This special group would be responsible for decisions about goals and their relative priority, although primarily a board level function administrative involvement is necessary where such decisions will affect program operations.

Auditing is an area where administrators lack knowledge. According to the Comptroller General of the United States, "The full scope of an audit of a governmental program, function, activity, or organization should encompass:

1. An examination of financial transactions, accounts, and reports, including an evaluation of compliance with applicable laws and regulations.
2. A review of efficiency and economy in the use of resources.
3. A review to determine whether desired results are effectively achieved.

In determining the scope for a particular audit, responsible officials should give consideration to the needs of the potential users of the results of the audit."[9]

Audit work is done by a certified public accountant or an independent public accountant and, upon completion, allows him to form an opinion on the fairness of the financial statements reported for the period. The accountant selectively tests transactions and internal controls, in effect from which he could verify the financial records and the reliability placed on the internal controls.[10]

An audit would be an extremely valuable asset and one method of evaluating program operations. It would provide insight relative to the accuracy of the reported financial statements and the proper use of resources and would help determine the extent to which results are being achieved and the reliability of an internal management information system.

GRANTSMANSHIP AND CONTRACTSMANSHIP

Fiscal management requires an understanding of the differences between contractsmanship and grantsmanship. Recent changes in federal and state policy place heavy emphasis on

---

[9]Comptroller General of the United States: *Standards for Audit of Governmental Organizations, Programs, Activities and Functions.* Washington, D.C., U.S. Government Printing Office, 1974 reprint, p. 10.
[10]For an excellent description of internal controls, *see* Gross, *Financial and Accounting Guide*, pp. 340-354.

contractsmanship, as in Title XX Programs and in some parts of drug and alcohol work. Administrators have had to shift accordingly.

A contract is basically an instrument used to procure research or services, whereas a grant is a mechanism to support research or services.[11] A contract is a legal agreement between two or more parties and is used to purchase an identified set of services or a defined product under specific conditions. Contracting also has an advantage of obtaining what is needed, where it is needed, and when it is needed, to the distinct economic advantage of the funding source. It is clearly an outgrowth of the accountability thrust and the public's emphasis on research which produces immediate and more practical results. A grant, on the other hand, is awarded by a funding source and generally supports ideas generated from the field. It offers greater flexibility and is used more to support basic research, where the researcher is concerned primarily with gaining a fuller knowledge of the idea under study and contributing to scientific knowledge.

A contract has the advantage of giving an agency more control over the work. The scope of services, the legally binding agreement as to what the contractee is to do, is more detailed and specific than that found in a grant. Moreover, if the contractee fails to do what is stated in the scope of services, the contractor does not have to pay for the work. As one observes, the scope of services demands much attention.

It is possible to obtain additional funds in a contractual arrangement. A contract is done for a certain amount of money. Baker points out that "if the work is completed for less than the contracted amount, the government keeps the difference. If . . . the investigator anticipates running out of money before the work is finished, he must notify the agency, which then has the option of taking everything done when the money runs out or of paying for the completion of the work — the infamous cost overrun."[12]

---

[11]Baker, Keith: The new contractsmanship. *The Grantsmanship Center News*, 2:21-27, 53-57, 1976.
[12]Baker, *Grantsmanship Center News*, p. 24.

There are two other important considerations in contractsmanship. First, the contractor and its contracting officer legally have complete control over the project. The contracting officer can make reasonable changes in the project without consulting the contractee. For example, if a contractee says that 100 tests are needed and the contracting officer says 50 is enough, the contracting officer's number is used.

The second consideration has to do with publishing a study under contract. Contracts generally call for reports written to the work specifications for use inside an agency. Contractees are usually bound by a copyright clause in which the agency retains exclusive rights to the data. Researchers interested in publications from the contract results must first secure the permission of the contractor or the contracting officer.

The advantages and control exercised in contracting should not go unnoticed by administrators. For example, in contracting for evaluation research, administrators need to appoint a contracting officer to work with researchers. They are then in an excellent position to specify the work involved and insure its quality. Few administrators take advantage of this opportunity at this time.

SOME USES OF BUDGETING

A budget is an organizational plan of financial action. It performs two basic functions. First, it identifies in monetary terms the direction of the program and is based on clear objectives emerging from the planning process. Second, budgets are excellent tools to monitor the financial activities throughout the year. Gross identifies four elements which are necessary for budgets to be used for monitoring purposes:

1. The budget must be well-conceived and been prepared or approved by the board.
2. The budget must be broken down into periods corresponding to the periodic financial statements.
3. Financial statements must be prepared on a timely basis throughout the year and a comparison made to the budget, written on the statements themselves.

4. The board must be prepared to take action where the comparison with the budget indicates a significant deviation.[13]

Administrators usually have no difficulty in preparing an annual budget and understanding that the budget presents program direction over the course of the budget. They encounter much difficulty in comparing the annual budget with the monthly and quarterly financial statements. Simply dividing the annual budget into twelve equal parts and showing the results on a monthly basis, which is then compared to actual monthly income and expense statements, can produce misleading conclusions when the income and expense vary throughout the year.

For example, assume that a program receives funds throughout the year in the following quarterly differentials: $40,000, $20,000, $20,000, and $40,000. Monthly comparisons by dividing the annual budget into twelve would suggest that the total of $120,000 would be distributed evenly throughout the year or $10,000 per month. Misleading conclusions can be made if in the second quarter only $20,000 in income is expected, although the budget assumption is that $30,000 is anticipated.

If budgets were prepared on a quarterly basis, deviations in actual income from anticipated income would be quickly noticed. Corrective management action could be taken early and before problems reached crisis proportions. In the above example, if one expects income of $40,000 in the first quarter and receives only $30,000, the financial discrepancy would be seen immediately, and management action would be required. The action might be to increase efforts to restore the $10,000 deficit or to revise the budget downward to the new annual figure. Nevertheless, the financial situation would be observed when it happens and when management action would have the best chance for success.

---

[13]Gross, *Financial and Accounting Guide*, p. 294.

FINANCIAL MANAGEMENT TECHNIQUES

Financial management techniques are designed with the intent to obtain the best service at the most feasible cost. This is done by conducting a systematic review and analysis of the work involved in delivering a certain service to clients. Each step of the process is assigned a value in monetary terms, and the total of all values becomes the cost for providing the service. Special attention must be given to identify the administrative work necessary to support and maintain the service, as these costs must also be included in the total cost of the service.

This type of analysis is intended to provide opportunities to reduce cost, such as streamlining the administrative work and eliminating some steps in service delivery. It can also expose gaps in service and provide the rationale for increasing cost along with improving service.

Financial management techniques are critical in contractsmanship and less crucial in grantsmanship. Grants normally have fixed awards and specified times when administrators can withdraw or draw down funds from the established account. Accounting responsibility emphasizes the keeping of records to show how the money was distributed and the accordance with program objectives.

In contracting, all parties negotiate cost, and contractees are awarded a maximum award relative to the number of people served or the amount of work completed. This is, in effect, the same as a voucher system where reimbursement occurs when a service is provided. For example, an agency may contract for providing 100 alcoholic clients with family services. It would receive money only in proportion to the number of people having actually received family services, and at the agreed rate of service per client. If 75 alcoholic clients receive family services, the agency would receive three-fourths of the maximum award.

While fiscal management is a major function of administration, the best that could be said about any one technique is that it too shall pass. The financial landscape is littered with the fallout from such techniques as the Planning-Program-Budgeting System (PPBS),[14] cost-benefit analysis,[15] and Program Evaluation and Review Technique (PERT).[16] The latest technique embraced by federal and state people is zero-based budgeting (ZBB),[17] and most assuredly another technique will take its place in the next few years.

Analyzing a program and its budget according to the format of any one of these techniques could be of substantial benefit to administrators, but completion of any one of these techniques will probably not result in an increase in program funds. Completing a program analysis according to the ZBB format will keep programs funded for another fiscal year. Use of any other technique at this time, no matter how enlightening, would be inappropriate and might result in a loss of funds. It is a matter of survival, for drug and alcohol programs receive an increase in funds based on political necessity and not because excellent plans were written or that financial management techniques were well done.

It is, therefore, important for administrators to develop a generic financial management system responsive to their decision-making needs. Such a system would be compatible with internal requirements and the external requirements of the various funding sources. It must possess stability and not be subject to wholesale changes when current financial management techniques are replaced.

For example, a generic financial management system might include and relate the organizational factors of identifying each service offered to clients, the manpower needs of each service,

[14]Lyden, Fremont J. and Miller, Ernest G. (Eds.): *Planning Programming Budgeting: A Systems Approach to Management.* Chicago, Markham, 1968.
[15]Hertzman, Marc and Montague, Barrie: Cost-benefit analysis and alcoholism. *Journal of Studies on Alcohol, 38*:1371-1385, 1977.
[16]Federal Electric Corporation: *A Programmed Introduction to PERT.* New York, Wiley, 1963.
[17]Pyhrr, Peter A.: *Zero Base Budgeting: A Practical Management Tool for Evaluating Expenses.* New York, Wiley, 1973; and Vignola, Margo L.: The latest in federal spending control: zero base budgeting. In Slavin, Simon (Ed.): *Social Administration.* New York, Haworth, 1978, pp. 293-298.

the identification of actual cost in the traditional categories of consultant services, travel, space and utilities, consumable supplies, rental or lease of equipment, etc., in relation to each service, and the output measures for each service.[18] This basic information when used in conjunction with the budget comparisons and financial statements suggested in other sections of this chapter would be of substantial benefit in decision making.

When using the form shown in Figure 8, specific services are identified, each service is assigned an account code identical to the bookkeeper's records, all direct and indirect costs in each category that are used to maintain and operate each service are totalled, and output measures for each service are identified. Cost per service would result from dividing one output measure into the total cost for that service. For example, one might list counseling, initial medical examination, and group therapy under program services and assign an account code to each, such as 1.0, 2.0, and 3.0.

Manpower needs for delivering the actual or direct service would be identified. Included would be all personnel that function in regard to a particular service. Obviously, counselors and their secretaries would be listed in relation to counseling, but counseling done by other personnel would be prorated and the cost added to the manpower category. Thus, if a nurse earns $10,000 annually and spends 20 percent of her time counseling patients, $2,000 of her wages would be applied to the manpower cost for delivering the counseling service.

Administrators must be certain to identify the cost of providing administrative services and apply them to each category for each service. These costs are considered as being indirect, for they go toward supporting the provision of each service. These costs will vary, and it is important to apply them appropriately, particularly in contracting when a cost per service figure is required. For example, obtaining consultant services

[18]The author expresses his appreciation to A. Billheimer of the Minneapolis Communication Center, Minneapolis, Minnesota, for his assistance in designing this form.

Drug and Alcohol Programs

SERVICE	ACCOUNT CODE	PERSONNEL	CONSULTANT CONTRACT SERVICE	TRAVEL	SPACE	
TOTAL PROJECT						

Figure 8. Cost Breakdown by Service.

	CONSUMABLE SUPPLIES	RENTAL OR LEASE OF EQUIPMENT	OTHER COSTS		TOTAL COST	OUTPUT MEASURES

Figure 8 (cont'd).

may require more administrative time and effort than ordering consumable supplies. Therefore, a smaller indirect cost would be applied to the cost for ordering supplies in regard to the particular service.

Direct and indirect costs are computed for each service and in each cost breakdown category. These costs are totalled and divided by the output measure for the service to obtain a cost per service figure. If the total cost for providing counseling services is $100,000, and the total number of counseling sessions made during the year is 10,000, the cost per counseling session is $10. Other output measures could be used, such as number of families served, but this would not affect the method of determining cost per service.

The major advantage in doing this type of financial management analysis is its applicability to meeting internal and external administrative requirements. In relation to ZBB, it would be easy to identify what could be done if a 10 percent budget increase or decrease were to result. Since cost and output measures are clearly identified, it would be possible to do a cost-benefit analysis. Moreover, each service has its own account code, and all business transactions would be coded at the time of posting. In this way actual costs can be compared with budget estimates, allowing fiscal decisions to be made intelligently.

Administrators should therefore not embrace any one technique and believe all problems will be solved. This is not to suggest that they may favor PERT or ZBB, but serve to remind them about political realities. Should financial management systems be based on ZBB, they would be inflexible when other techniques are used. In these instances systems must be completely reworked, resulting in an almost constant state of reorganization and retraining. Consequently, more time and effort would go toward keeping pace with the changes at the expense of effective and stable management.

INTERDISCIPLINARY COLLABORATION AND CONSULTANTS

One of the key abilities administrators of drug and alcohol

programs must possess is being able to mediate the differences between the various disciplines operating in the context of the organization. Schein observes that the various functions which make up an organization are always mediated by the interactions of people so that the organization can never escape its human processes.[19] When groups of people who represent many different professions interact in one organization, it is inevitable that conflicts will arise. These conflicts form the substance of much administrative activity.

Interdisciplinary collaboration occurs when different professions interact either inside or outside the organization. Inside organizations, administrators are called upon to insure that this collaborative effort proceeds with recognition for service to the client. It is very easy for professionals to use the clients as a medium for acting out their own differences. For example, it has been observed on several occasions that guidance counselors, social workers, paraprofessionals, psychologists, and nurses, in trying to demonstrate their special therapeutic competency, will overlook the client problems in team meetings.

The team meeting is another area to observe interdisciplinary collaboration in action. This term is usually applied to all situations where the various professionals discuss clients, and it implies a certain degree of equality. In the drug and alcohol field, as in medicine, there is no equality when an individual is under the care of a physician. The physician is the real leader of the team, although one may be more influenced at times by other members.

Administrators are required constantly to find the common ground for the various disciplines to display their competence. One such common ground is found when the focus is on *the problem*. Various professionals can be expected to define the problem according to their view, often excluding the client's view, and it is not unusual for professionals to disagree about the definition of the problem. Sharp administrators usually recognize this situation when it happens, and if recognition fails to bring accord, they would be wise to follow the client's definition when action is taken.

---

[19]Schein, Edgar H.: *Process Consultation: Its Role in Organization Development.* Reading, Md., Addison-Wesley, 1969.

Interdisciplinary collaboration outside the organization typically involves the development of coalitions or associations. Coalitions tend to be used in relation to a specific problem, particularly when a large number of people or organizations are affected. After the perceived threat is lessened, the coalition dissolves or evolves into a more permanent organization. An association is one such organization, and it soon develops as a separate entity, responding to its specialized constituency and the maintenance of its own objectives. For example, program administrators might find it highly appropriate to get together in response to proposed budget cuts. After several meetings their original purpose may no longer exist, yet they continue meeting. In a short time an association of program administrators would be formed, and it would also respond to many other issues pertaining to the interests of the program administrators.

A major problem in interdisciplinary collaboration is language. Each profession has developed its own jargon to describe behavior. Unless there is a mechanism by which each group's jargon is translated across professional boundaries, the total perspective for understanding clients and their behavior will continue to be fragmented. Professionals often need to learn how to talk amongst themselves and to clients in terms all can understand. Administrators should insist that this happen.

USE OF CONSULTANTS

Administrators may find consultants to be particularly helpful in interdisciplinary collaboration. They can serve in a more objective role and presumably have greater interest in achieving stated objectives. For example, administrators can develop or help to implement solutions to thorny problems. Their presence often serves to remove the total responsibility for recommendations for action from people inside the organization.

Consultants are also able to provide a range of other services to organizations. They can identify problems in structural, management, and administrative policies and operations as well as in substantive program areas; they can do training or orientation sessions; they can do research and evaluation studies; and they can assist in identifying and mobilizing local, state, and federal funding sources. Each service requires administrators to know precisely what they want to achieve so as to make the best use of consultants.

Consultants can be used to introduce innovation and bring about organizational change. They often bring fresh ideas to a more stale situation and, through the use of recommendations, can effect organizational change. Consultants can recommend changes more easily because their status places them outside the daily context of organizational politics. They are perceived to be more objective.

Determining the objectives for consultant use is one step in the entire process of employing consultants. Other steps include identifying and assessing the various consultant sources, insuring that contracts and contract procurement procedures are followed, making preparations to use the consultant, insuring proper on-site utilization of the consultant, and deciding if, and how many, follow-up activities are needed.

Consultants may be identified from many sources. Funding agencies, other programs, colleagues, and consultants themselves are the usual sources to tap for this information. Contract development normally requires legal assistance, with the scope of services and special arrangements being supplied by the administrator.

It is important to make preparations for using consultants. Administrators may want to review these preparations to guarantee that the consultant's time is scheduled appropriately, that key people have been notified of the consultant's visit, that needed material has been distributed, and that any special arrangements have been made.

Of special concern would be the on-site utilization of the consultant. The administrator should brief consultants at the onset of the contract and hold regular meetings throughout the length of the contract. Work space, supplies, and clerical support should be clarified prior to the consultant's arrival.

Effective consultation is predicated on administrators knowing the objectives for such assistance. There are times when consultants are imposed on programs and proceed to define their role in the organization for the administrator. This is common in the drug and alcohol field because of the lack of adequately trained administrators. In such a situation, funding sources define organizational problems, procure consultants, and contract with them to provide technical assistance to drug and alcohol programs. Although consultation has long been available, its potential was never fully realized, in part because program people resented the imposition of external *experts* and, in part, due to the organization not being fully convinced it *owned* the already defined problem. Competent management would help to overcome this situation and allow for effective use of consultants.

SUMMARY

This chapter explores the many dimensions of planning and planning-related activities. Planning is oversold as a panacea of organizational problems and social ills, and it is viewed from a more restrictive perspective. Distinctions were made between administration and planning, a plan and a planning process, and the nature and complexity of planning at local, state, and federal levels. Each distinction was discussed as it impacted on administration, especially the need for an administrative-oriented planning process.

The organization of services in the drug and alcohol field was presented from a model based on prevention, secondary, and tertiary categories. Most program activity occurs in the tertiary or treatment category followed by prevention activities. Merged treatment programs are discussed infrequently in the literature, despite the extent of mixing drug and alcohol clients in the field.

Fiscal management is seen as the hub of administration, and usually administrators need assistance in accounting, in skillful budgeting, in contract cost specification, and in keeping pace with changing financial management techniques for analyzing their budget.

Administrative skill was seen as necessary in interdisciplinary collaboration to mediate the differences between various professional and paraprofessional groups. The roles of consultants were explained, both inside and outside the organization, and the steps for involving them in organizations were identified.

Chapter 7

RESEARCH AND EVALUATION ISSUES

R ESEARCH and evaluation has become a significant requirement at practically all levels of program operation. Community mental health centers, for example, have been mandated to spend around 2 percent of their operating budget for research and evaluation efforts. In this age of extreme accountability, the many publics clamor for program studies indicating what programs are doing and the extent to which program objectives are being achieved.

In view of all the public attention and practical requirements, it is somewhat surprising that research and evaluation remains one area of administrative responsibility which seems to be surrounded by an air of intellectual mystique. Far too often administrators leave almost total responsibility for this important task in the hands of researchers. This chapter is intended to demystify the research and evaluation process, thereby providing encouragement for administrators to retain more control and direction over this area of management.

There are several key areas which need to be clarified if one is to demystify the research and evaluation process. It seems logical that attention be focused on understanding the research process itself, identifying the major parts of a research effort, learning which type of research is most helpful to administrators, clarifying some of the political implications of evaluation studies, and providing a basis for assessing existing research in the drug and alcohol field.

UNDERSTANDING THE RESEARCH PROCESS

One of the major problems in understanding the research process is that people do not conduct social research according to the way it is written in books or the way it is usually taught. In books on research one is presented with generalized principles pertaining to the conduct of research under idealized circumstances. The research process is generally conceived as including the following aspects:[1]

1. The statement and formulation of the problem which needs to be studied.
2. The review of any literature considered relevant to the problem.
3. The development of a research design to answer questions posed in the problem statement.
4. The selection of data collection techniques and procedures.
5. The processing and analyzing of the obtained data in relation to research hypotheses.
6. The writing of the report indicating conclusions and interpretations of the research.

Unfortunately, this idealized research process is not the way the actual study is conducted. Social researchers simply cannot plan and conduct research without considering the impact of a host of personal, organizational, and community factors on each step of the entire study. Hence, administrators need to be cautious when they hear researchers talk about conducting research using the classical experimental design without giving much attention to the significant social factors which impinge upon any social research effort.

One requirement for the conduct of research and evaluation efforts would obviously be that the scientific method be followed. This method would minimally include the previously identified aspects for conducting research. Due to a desired emphasis on program issues and the relationship of practice and policy, it seems evident that research be conducted in field or community settings. Social research would then be defined as "the systematic application of logical strategies and observational techniques for purposes of developing, modifying, and expanding knowledge about social phenomena."[2]

Social research also covers medical research done in the field.

---

[1]Tripodi, Tony: *Uses and Abuses of Social Research in Social Work.* New York, Columbia, 1974, p. 11.

[2]Tripodi, *Uses and Abuses of Social Research*, p. 18.

The central issue is that when any study is conducted outside of a laboratory setting, or any setting where factors are difficult to control, the impact of social forces needs to be considered. Although methadone treatment protocols were designed according to appropriate scientific concerns, one could not keep methadone patients from talking among themselves about the effects of the drug on their bodies. This is just one situation where social factors in the field will tend to affect practically all research designs.

One of the more technical parts of research is its design. Its scientific character and specialized technology tend to convince administrators that they should refer this matter to the experts. The research design is basically the plan by which the researcher will conduct the study, and administrators can relate themselves to the notion of a plan. In drug and alcohol research three types of research design or plan are most appropriate — single subject, longitudinal, and survey.

Single subject or case study designs begin by studying individuals in order to discover valid principles for explaining the behavior of each.[3] It is exploratory research, and individuals, groups, or organizations are selected specifically because they possess particular problems. They are usually treated as co-investigators, as active participants, or as expert consultants. Control conditions are not important, as key variables are sought and described. Through repeated single case studies, validation of findings may be obtained. Such studies are published when innovative procedures are demonstrated or when results obtained from a sufficient number of subjects lend themselves to generality. Essentially, one would use this design to derive hypotheses for further testing or to develop research priorities.

The longitudinal design is more conventionally used in research. In simple longitudinal designs, individuals are sampled from some target population and measured repeatedly on two

[3]Shontz, Franklin C.: Single-organism designs. In Bentler, Peter M., Lettieri, Dan J., and Austin, Gregory A. (Eds.): *Data Analysis Strategies and Designs for Substance Abuse Research.* Rockville, Md., NIDA, 1976, pp. 25-44.

or more occasions.[4] It should be rather clear that any social intervention aimed at modifying human behavior requires measurements of change within and between individuals over time, or a longitudinal design. But such studies require much time and effort on the part of both researchers and subjects, which is why short-term studies of a cross-sectional target population have been favored.

In longitudinal design the strategy of experimentation is employed to learn whether a causal relationship exists between two variables, one being designated as the independent and the other the dependent. The independent or causal variable is assumed to bring about the desired effect (dependent variable), occurs in time prior to the outcome, and is solely responsible (no other variables or factors are responsible) for the observed changes in the dependent variable. In drug research, to test the assertion that encounter group therapy (independent variable) for heroin addicts leads to a reduction in criminal activity (dependent variable), it is necessary to show that (1) a reduction in criminal activity actually occurs in the population receiving the encounter group treatment, (2) the reduction in criminal activity occurs after the encounter group treatment is employed, and (3) other variables, such as individual counseling, are not responsible for the observed outcome in criminal activity.

Surveys are undertaken for descriptive or exploratory purposes.[5] In both situations the same research strategy is used, except in the exploratory survey procedures are also used to compare contrasting populations, and statistical methods are employed to determine relationships between variables.

Descriptive surveys are most familiar to administrators. They are used typically to provide descriptions of opinions and to determine the needs of people in the community, the extent to which people use drug and alcohol facilities, and what people might think about a specific project, etc. Since they tap attitu-

---

[4]Labouvie, Erich W.: Longitudinal designs. In Bentler, Peter M., Lettieri, Dan J., and Austin, Gregory A. (Eds.): *Data Analysis Strategies and Designs for Substance Abuse Research*. Rockville, Md., NIDA, 1976, pp. 45-60.
[5]Tripodi, *Uses and Abuses of Social Research*, pp. 22-26.

dinal responses, caution must be used in extending the survey results beyond their capabilities. Survey results are not able to predict accurately what people will actually do in certain situations, nor can one identify why people answered the way that they did.

Administrators must be certain that any research and evaluation effort demonstrates the application of the scientific method to the field or agency situation. Research proposals which do not address directly the impact of social factors on the research process ought to be discarded or returned for clarification. Administrators might choose to also question researchers at length about some problems they might expect in the research process, for reasons of personal enlightenment as well as organizational necessity. They must hold researchers accountable for the kind of research produced and require them to describe clearly the methodology used, with explicit definitions of all concepts, terms, techniques, and procedures employed in the study. A good rule-of-thumb would be for administrators to determine if they could replicate the study from the researchers report. If replication is not possible, they should require researchers to rewrite the report.

RESEARCH ETHICS

A recent concern has centered on human subject considerations in all research efforts. Administrators in methadone programs will quickly recognize how much energy was devoted to the development and implementation of an informed consent procedure, which has since been expanded to include other program areas. University-based researchers must now have research involving human subjects reviewed by their peers for ethical violations.

Administrators are in an excellent position to monitor and insure that the interests of the subjects are maintained. Confidentiality can be as much a problem in research as in treatment. Insuring that research data be accessible to only identified personnel and be kept in safe areas would quickly demonstrate that a high degree of ethical integrity is being maintained.

Most important is for administrators to be vigorous and consistent with the researchers and the study participants. One may get trapped easily in research endeavors and overlook some ethical considerations because all those involved may believe they have the subject's interest at heart. Should research efforts result in subjects developing negative attitudes, there most certainly will be program problems for administrators to face. It would be wise and prudent for administrators to continue monitoring all research efforts in their agency, in addition to securing all documents related to informed consent. In short, just because it is written does not mean it will be followed.

The most important issue in safeguarding the interest of subjects is informed consent. In general, informed consent has been regarded as a benchmark of ethical human experimentation. However, truly informed consent is a very difficult condition to attain; and, in some situations, particularly in biomedical research, complete disclosure of a study's detail may invalidate it.[6] Administrators need to insure that these two conditions not be violated and make every effort to obtain full disclosure and truly informed consent in all instances.

There are times when, despite clear statements, some people will think differently. For example, administrators should recognize that an individual's right to treatment is separate from participation in research. Statements to this effect may be stated clearly on the informed consent form, and this may be reinforced at various points throughout the study. Yet some subjects may feel and believe that their participation places them in a position different from similar people in the agency. In such instances, the research program has to be analyzed carefully to ascertain if participants are indeed benefiting from any unintended consequences or are being deprived of certain advantages.

DISTINCTIONS BETWEEN RESEARCH
AND EVALUATION STUDIES

Evaluation research is the most appropriate type of research

---

[6]Thomas, Lewis: The benefits of research. In *Experiments and Research with Humans: Values in Conflict*. Washington, D.C., National Academy of Sciences, 1975, pp. 31-35.

for use by administrators in the drug and alcohol field. Evaluation research is similar to all other types of research. It has no special methodology. The scientific method applies, and researchers use the same research methods to collect and analyze data. The classic design for conducting evaluations has been based on the experimental model, with evaluation striving for describing and understanding the relationships between variables. In short, the same format used for other research is used for evaluation studies.

The differences between evaluation and other research make evaluation research highly appropriate for administrators. Evaluation is applied social or administrative research. It takes place in an action setting, where clients are being served or where the most important activity is the program. Its study population consists normally of a direct consumer group, which are those people about to be, have been, or are being served or affected by a particular program or agency.

In addition, the purpose and object of evaluation research is significantly different from other research. Weiss notes that it is intended for use and is usually aimed at effective action.[7] People who have decisions to make look to evaluation for answers on which to base their decisions. On the other hand, the major purpose of basic research is to verify the existence of a relationship between variables and places emphasis on the production of knowledge. The utilization of research is usually left to others for dissemination and application.

Suchman indicates that another difference is the form taken by the statement of the problem:

> Essential to basic research is the formulation of a nonevaluative hypothesis relating two variables in a "the more (a), the more (b) format". . . . There is no implication about the desirability or undesirability of (b) or about the possibility of manipulating (a). In evaluation research . . . the effect (b) becomes the valued or desired goal of some program (a) which is deliberately designed to change (b). Whereas "pure" science asks the question, Is it a fact that (a) is related to (b)?, and

---

[7]Weiss, Carol H.: *Evaluation Research*. Englewood Cliffs, N.J., Prentice-Hall, 1972, pp. 1-10.

then proceeds to test the "truth" of this relationship by means of experimental or field designs which attempt to hold other possible "causes" constant, "applied" science asks, Does (a) work effectively to change (b)?, and attempts to answer this question empirically by setting up a program which manipulates (a) and then measuring the effect on (b).[8]

Other differences have been noted by several authors. These differences are program-derived questions.[9] judgmental quality,[10] and role conflicts.[11] The differences probably arise more from the distinctions already mentioned than by the research process itself. For example, judgmental quality refers to the aspect of evaluation which compares *what is* with *what should be* and may be reflected in the way the questions for study are formulated.[12] Role conflicts would also seem to be an inherent part of the evaluation process as practitioners and evaluators alike focus on a specific program, the practitioners usually committed to the worth of the program they are providing and the evaluators weighing the merits of practitioner activities.

PROBLEMS IN CONDUCTING STUDIES

The very nature of doing a study can be problematic for administrators. Several distinctions between basic and applied evaluative research efforts can prove to pose serious difficulties in the conduct of research. Several such problems are highlighted to alert administrators to the fact that any research effort requires as much attention as other program efforts. The consequences of poor research strategies can effectively serve to affect adversely and sometimes destroy the positive effects of

[8]Suchman, Edward A.: *Evaluation Research: Principles and Practice in Public Service and Social Action Programs.* New York, Russell Sage, 1967, pp. 78-79.
[9]Twain, David: Developing and implementing a research strategy. In Struening, Elmer L. and Guttentag, Marcia (Eds.): *Handbook of Evaluation Research.* Vol. I. New York, Russell Sage, 1975, pp. 27-52; and Weiss, *Evaluation Research,* p. 6.
[10]Weiss, *Evaluation Research,* pp. 24-59.
[11]Aronson, Sidney H. and Sherwood, Clarence C.: Researcher versus practitioner: Problems in social action research. In Weiss, Carol H. (Ed.): *Evaluating Action Programs.* Boston, Allyn & Bacon, 1972, pp. 283-293.
[12]Weiss, *Evaluation Research,* p. 6.

other program areas.

Researchers have interests different from practitioners. Their interests lie in the conduct of research, the search for answers to problems, asking which treatment methods work best, and in communicating learned knowledge to a broader audience. Practitioners are concerned with obtaining specific answers to their questions, tend to be firmly committed to a certain treatment method, are less interested in adhering to the requirements of proper research, and are most interested in how to get things done. These differences are an inherent strain in the researcher-practitioner relationship, and one must learn how to minimize any negative effects arising from their interaction. This is a task for administrators.

Another task would be to mediate any differences emerging from research activities done in an organization. Administrators realize fully that changes in program operations will occur regardless of the size of a study. These changes are most common in an increased use of forms, a necessary requirement for obtaining data. But changes can also occur in treatment procedures, reporting requirements, and in management. One must be prepared to respond to the natural hesitation for engaging in research which often alters staff behavior. Weiss feels that the "use of evaluation appears to be easiest when implementation implies only moderate alteration in procedure, staff deployment, or costs, or where few interests are threatened."[13] These conditions cannot be met easily.

Worthwhile research and evaluation efforts need the support and attention of administrators. One should not even consider engaging in research endeavors if a strong commitment is lacking. It should not be assumed that competent researchers can fill this gap. Competent researchers can do their job well, but they are not involved directly in the supervisory chain of command and do not have any authority over workers. An administrator may find it necessary to intervene and support the research activity over staff protest. This requires commitment.

---

[13]Weiss, Carol H.: Utilization of evaluation: Toward comparative study. In Weiss, Carol H. (Ed.): *Evaluating Action Programs.* Boston, Allyn & Bacon, 1972, p. 320.

The key to resolving or minimizing problems in this as well as in other research areas is for the administrator to be the central figure and decision maker. An example situation would be if the staff reports a fear of driving clients away from treatment, and they ask if they should continue to inundate clients with completing forms before being seen. The concern may have some merit as the administrator realizes that the time period could take about one hour. The project could become viewed as a source of paperwork, particularly since the staff might perceive greater benefits coming from other efforts. In order to deal effectively with staff concerns, administrators need to relate staff concerns to the purpose of the research and its various aspects. Appeals to the value and importance of research or restating the researchers' interests will likely not be heard.

Finally, administrators must clearly expect problems in the actual research activity to occur regardless of preplanning. Funds may be reduced, subjects may not be easily located, researchers and staff may leave the positions, or tentative findings may pose problems for the funding source or the agency. Each of these problems will necessitate managerial action, and one should expect them to occur rather than be surprised when they do appear.

BENEFITS OF KNOWING THE RESEARCH PROCESS

While it is not imperative for administrators to have conducted research projects themselves, understanding the various aspects of the entire evaluation research process can provide them with some important benefits. These benefits bear mentioning because they would solidify the rationale and emphasize the importance of research in administrative practice.

First, evaluation research can support a thrust for improved management by its contribution to rational decision making. It is a way to increase the rationality of policy and decision making because it is research designed for use by decision makers, its questions are derived from program people, and its focus is often on program effectiveness, which is a crucial concern to decision makers.

Evaluation research is a scientific process that takes place in a political context.[14] Drug and alcohol programs tend to be creatures of political decisions, and evaluations are undertaken normally to feed into the decision-making process. The questions posed for study and the evaluation itself are both political in character. Thus, the evaluation study must include many other factors such as public receptivity, costs, and participant reaction before findings become facts.

Evaluation research can provide data that reduce uncertainties and clarify the gains and losses that different decisions incur. The degree of objectivity in the research process, the political context of the study itself, and the consideration of other factors in addition to outcome evidence all tend to support a more thoughtful consideration of various alternatives. This is not to imply that evaluation research is a panacea for decision makers, but rather to illustrate that the nature of evaluation research is the most compatible type of research for administrative concerns.

Knowledge of the research and evaluation process would make it possible for administrators to handle any difficult situations. Already discussed has been administrative support, but other steps can be taken. Administrators can identify points where practitioners can be involved in the evaluation. This would be very helpful in the drug and alcohol field where speculation and suspicion are ever present and where evaluation is in a highly charged political context.

Other actions would be to reduce the strain on staff by hiring research assistants to work on evaluation tasks, to recognize when certain tasks would impose heavier demands than appear necessary, such as the length of an interview schedule or the number of tests to be administered, and to clarify continually

---

[14]Cohen, David K.: Politics and research: Evaluation of social action programs in education. In Weiss, Carol H. (Ed.): *Evaluating Action Programs*. Boston, Allyn & Bacon, 1972, pp. 137-165; and Weiss, Carol H.: The politicization of evaluation research. *Journal of Social Issues, XXVI*:57-68, 1970; and Weiss, Carol H.: Evaluation research in the political context. In Struening, Elmer L. and Guttentag, Marcia (Eds.): *Handbook of Evaluation Research*. Vol. I. New York, Russell Sage, 1975, pp. 13-21.

the various roles of people involved in the evaluation.[15] Administrative foresight would help minimize the severity of problems which if left unattended could place more stress on the tenuous practitioner-researcher relationship.

Feedback is very important. On several occasions otherwise well-conceived evaluation projects have faltered because staff had received no information as to the status of the project, especially if they invested much effort. Feedback can be valuable in making corrections in regard to certain problems, can encourage staff in that their efforts have been used, and can give the evaluation a more human quality.

There might be instances when evaluation efforts may be viewed personally. Although one might be out to discover more than whether certain treatment methods work best in this agency with this staff in this particular time and with these clients, the message may not be clearly heard. It is sometimes helpful to constantly relate the subject matter to the general context of theory. Widening the perspective may serve to at least lessen any perceived threats.

Probably most benefit could be obtained in the areas of leadership and contracting. By being knowledgeable, anticipating that certain problems will emerge, and talking with staff and evaluators, administrators will be perceived in a leadership position. The administrator can announce that he/she is the boss, but it requires practical demonstration to this effect to fully realize the role. Should any grievances or questions arise, as one would expect, it should be very clear to all whom they must contact.

Finally, developing the research project will enable administrators to better negotiate the scope of services, cost, and all other aspects of the research and evaluation process. They would not be easily deceived and could raise legitimate questions for evaluators' consideration before any repercussions occur. Indeed, knowing what to ask and then to ask is far superior to not being able to even formulate any questions.

---

[15]Weiss, *Evaluation Research,* pp. 104-107.

POLITICAL IMPLICATIONS

The emphasis on evaluation and evaluative research highlights the political nature of social research in general. Applied evaluative research is designed for use by decision makers for it can yield conclusions about the worth of a program. When various social programs compete for public funds in a political arena, at a time when the pool of money is not increasing, outcome becomes a major consideration. People will want to know what they are purchasing for their money and, more importantly, if their dollars are achieving the kind of outcome or result they expect.

Persons working with drug and alcohol related problems have always had to concern themselves with the political nature of their programs. For example, it is still not apparent what the real intent is of methadone treatment programs. The dilemma over whether its purpose is to help heroin addicts or to keep them from committing crimes is not just rhetorical. As a medication, methadone apparently did its job, but it had absolutely no effect on the social problems surrounding the treated individual. Counselors were still not able to secure employment for most treated people, nor were they able to help many clients overcome the effects of institutional racism. Administrators therefore had to always be cognizant of the political ramifications of their programs.

Program staff have become increasingly aware of the political nature of evaluations. Never really excited about participating in research efforts, they look with suspicion at evaluators who poke around, not sure of how the data will be used. They are quick to make their own inferences about all types of data. Program staff will usually try to present data most favorable to themselves or to their agency, or they may restrict access to certain data.

Evaluation studies have perhaps their greatest impact on funding sources. When applying for new or additional monies it can be very helpful to report some positive results from program or organizational efforts. Unfortunately, many reports indicate only few positive effects from diverse program areas, such as psychotherapy, education, and casework, causing Weiss to note that "to judge from evaluations, most action programs do not make much change in the behavior of individuals and groups."[16] In the political context, administrators need to work with evaluators throughout the study to learn how they can best use the findings for their purposes. They may have the most control over a project conducted.

The question of which people are best able to conduct evaluation efforts is sometimes the subject of much debate. Naturally, inhouse or outside evaluations each have advantages and disadvantages, and to administrators goes the task of reaching a decision. Some obvious factors to be considered are the purpose of the study, how it is expected to be used, confidence in evaluators, and the source of funds.

The purpose of the study is crucial. If one wants to explore ways to reorganize an agency or do comparisons of program treatment modalities, then outside evaluators may be the most appropriate alternative, due to their objectivity. Inhouse staff may be better suited to evaluation efforts that describe programs or explore specific treatment methods. It is best generally to use outside evaluators if objectivity is important to overcome vested interests.

How one expects the research findings to be used should be considered along with purpose. Does one want to learn about treatment? Does one want to secure funds? Does one want to confirm certain decisions? These questions imply the presence of at least two audiences, i.e. administrators and the target population or group of people to whom the findings might have greatest appeal. Thus, the use of evaluators would also have to be considered from the context of the targeted population. For example, governing bodies are likely to give greater weight to outside evaluations over inhouse evaluations.

One must have confidence in evaluators and their skill. These are two different factors, and administrators might choose to respond accordingly. Competence in evaluation skills does not automatically mean confidence in the person possessing them. Personality compatibility between the evaluator,

---

[16]Weiss, *Journal of Social Issues,* p. 62.

the administrators, the staff, and the clients is often significant. Obviously, some agency people are impressed with academic credentials and reputations of certain individuals, and these should be considered in the context of the target population. For example, it would be prudent to obtain the services of a certain evaluator, if it is also known that the evaluator is viewed favorably by the funding sources to which one intends to submit a proposal. It may be as important to purchase the political context of evaluators as well as their skill.

A fourth consideration would be the source of funds. Some programs do have research and evaluation inhouse capabilities. Most programs do not, which then have no choice and must always use outsiders for evaluations. Moreover, at times they may not even have the luxury of selecting the outside evaluator, as this selection may be done by a parent organization or their funding source.

When agencies are able to select evaluators, one key factor would be the availability of funds. Use of outside evaluators may require a realignment of program dollars, the use of an already existing account, or solicitation for grant or contract dollars. When agencies are not able to select evaluators, or perhaps only have a chance to participate in the selection process, its interest would be best served by exploring other factors in depth while pressing for how payment will occur. Should some evaluation dollars be applied to the agency's account or come directly from program funds, administrators might be able to obtain a greater voice as well as keep abreast of program changes.

INFORMATION SYSTEMS

Information systems may be viewed as part of the research and evaluation effort. They are systematic efforts directed toward the accumulation of data for rather diverse purposes. Their differences are found in usage since information systems are used to collect and retain data for diverse purposes by planners, administrators, researchers, and other policy makers.

Information systems in the drug and alcohol field are still an untapped excellent source of support for administrators. Practically all systems in use today are designed in response to the completion of necessary reporting forms for sources external to the organization, such as federal, state, and local agencies and private foundations. Such systems define the needs of the externally based organization, and the data is programmed accordingly. This type of information system does not respond to the internal decision-making needs of drug and alcohol programs.

Administrators must start designing information systems relative to decision-making situations to meet both internal and external requirements. The major problem in the past has been that they simply are unable to clarify their administrative information needs, an important skill given the present management situation in the field. This section is intended to help clarify some of those requirements for better management by exploring the types of information needed at three levels — the general, the client, and administrative.

The general level of information refers to the kind gathered to assess the impact of many programs on society and to make program comparisons in such areas as treatment outcome and budget. All federal and state reporting systems are included in this category. The evaluation data required typically are employment, education or training, arrest record, and amount of substance abuse and are applied uniformly to all funded projects by the funding source.

Information at the general level may be also considered as standards by which program comparisons can be made at the local, state, and federal levels. Program indicators such as budget and staffing patterns provide quick and easy access to important structural data, and when these indicators are incorporated with client-related data, the outcome can be quite significant. Administrators generally do not have accessibility to this kind of information and tend to have concerns about its use. When compared with other programs, one can easily surmise the impact on the administration of any program should it learn that its costs are higher or that it is ranked near or at the bottom of certain lists.

While the general level of information accounts for certain

client characteristics, dispositions, program assignments, budget, staffing patterns, and some outcomes, it does not focus on the qualities of the treatment process itself. General level information may reveal poor results for a clinic or a specific modality, but it is not able to define the parts of a facility's program needing improvement. Information obtained from the client system level of reporting would allow one to analyze the treatment process in sufficient detail to permit the making of pertinent recommendations to administrators.

Client system data provides for more complete program assessments to be made. One can view the outcome or products at the general level in terms of a box where all that is being measured is what goes in (input) and what comes out (output). The specific nature of the box (the facility or program) is basically unknown. Client system data enables one to look inside the box by examining process variables and determine what actually happens during the treatment process of the facility or program.

The type of information needed in the client system would fall into two categories.[17] Descriptive information pertaining to the program background, the clients, the staff, and fiscal concerns can be utilized as a basis for summarizations in this category. Analytic information of both a quantitative and qualitative nature would comprise the second category. Staff-to-client and counselor-to-client ratios, staff turnover rate, and cost per client per year form a minimum basis of quantitative information, while the quality of records, the continuity and completeness of records, how often clients are exposed to particular treatment services, and the validity and reliability of reported data will serve to qualify and measure the treatment process.

Administrative information systems are very different from the other two levels of information. These systems incorporate the requirements of a general and client nature, but address the needs of administrators in planning, decision making, and control. Such systems are oriented toward management and are

---

[17]*See,* for example, the Commonwealth of Pennsylvania Governor's Council on Drug and Alcohol Abuse data report forms.

invaluable in reaching decisions.

Management considerations cover more than the treatment process. Changes in the dispensing of drugs, the cost of office and janitorial supplies, the number of clients seen in treatment, and every part of the program or facility need to be monitored closely. Once a normal level of output is achieved, changes on a daily or weekly basis would signal a note of caution. Upon investigation into the reasons for such changes, administrators would be able to determine what, if any, corrective management action need to be taken.

The form of information most useful in this category is grouped data. Singular pieces of information, such as the contact between a counselor and a client, need to be combined for administrative purposes. Grouped data can indicate the extent to which certain situations are prevalent, whereas singular data would not be helpful. For example, a counselor may inform an administrator that two clients have difficulty with a particular action. The administrator would be unable to reach any decision until information is obtained from other counselors on the number of clients also having the same trouble. In essence, problems experienced by only 2 or 50 out of 100 clients might require that different decisions be made.

ASSESSMENT OF TREATMENT RESEARCH

Competent management also implies keeping abreast of current treatment research. Treatment outcomes are, after all, the most visible product of drug and alcohol programs. Administrators need to know what is flowing from treatment research so they can plan accordingly.

Much of the emphasis in assessing treatment research is on alcoholism, built on well over half a century of study. Studies of drug treatment have been reported in significant numbers only since the early 1970s, and hardly any studies have been done on combined drug and alcohol clients. Moreover, the addictive process is generally applicable to the drug and alcohol abusers, although there may be differences in such things as the reasons for abuse and motivation for being in treatment and recovery. Thus, one could assess treatment research with more confidence from primarily an alcoholism perspective.

Periodically during the past forty years excellent articles that review the efficacy of alcoholism treatment have appeared in the literature. In each of these reviews, criteria are presented by which the studies under scrutiny are judged. The criteria vary, of course, according to the writer's orientation, but nevertheless all essentially reach the same conclusion. This conclusion is that few acceptable research designs have been carried out which would yield valuable scientific information despite, as Mandell states, "excellent articles published periodically reviewing the faults of previous studies and pointing clearly to what needs to be done in the way of research methodology."[18]

In 1942, Voegtlin and Lemere reviewed over 200 publications from 1901 to 1941 which purported to evaluate any form of treatment for alcoholics.[19] They were interested in evidence of treatment outcomes. Instead they repeatedly found an almost complete lack of outcome data as well as a lack of any clearly identified cure or outcome measures.

Hill and Blane in 1967 selected five requirements of evaluative research and analyzed forty-nine studies published in the United States and Canada from 1952 to 1963.[20] Their five requirements are use of controls, subject selection procedures, selection of and definition of criterion variables, measurement instruments, and their reliability and measurement before and after treatment. Data collection methods were generally found to be so inept that no reliance could be placed on the reported findings.

Pattison did a critique of alcoholism treatment concepts with special reference to abstinence in 1966 and concluded that "clinical experience and research data demonstrate that the models employed in defining and evaluating alcoholism treat-

---

[18]Mandell, Wallace: Does the type of treatment make a difference? Paper presented to the American Society on Alcoholism, 1971, p. 1.

[19]Voegtlin, W. L. and Lemere, F.: The treatment of alcohol addiction: A review of the literature. *Quarterly Journal of Studies on Alcohol, 2*:717-803, 1942.

[20]Hill, Marjorie J. and Blane, Howard T.: Evaluation of psychotherapy with alcoholics. *Quarterly Journal of Studies on Alcohol, 28*:76-104, 1967.

ment require modification."[21] In effect, these three literature reviews concluded that no reliable conclusions can be made about treatment results.

In 1977, Crawford and Chalupsky did a methodological review of forty journal articles reporting treatment evaluations for the years 1968 to 1971.[22] Their findings were a bit more encouraging but agreed with the conclusions of previous literature reviews. They reported finding a number of studies that dealt "thoughtfully and competently with particular issues."[23] However, "the median level of effort remains at such a relatively unsophisticated level that most studies were both scientifically and practically unproductive."[24]

It would appear helpful to identify and briefly discuss some of the major criteria used to analyze evaluative studies. Administrators should note the utility of such criteria in conducting their own literature reviews and analyzing each study, including those done on their own agencies. The major criteria are control conditions, identifying and defining the independent variable, identifying and defining the dependent variable, and the procedure and measurement technique used to obtain and analyze the data.

In research, a control condition is established so that one can compare one individual or group who possesses or has received the *thing* or *variable* to be studied with another individual or group lacking the same *thing* or *variable*. Alcohol or drug research on the efficacy of treatment would suggest the establishment of a group which receives treatment and a group which does not receive the same treatment. It is this issue which seems most problematic since one cannot ethically or politically deny treatment to a certain group of people in need of treatment, nor is one able to establish a pure control group, as might be anticipated in randomly assigning patients to specific

[21]Pattison, E. M.: A critique of alcoholism treatment concepts with special reference to abstinence. *Quarterly Journal of Studies on Alcohol, 27*:1966, p. 56.

[22]Crawford, Jack J. and Chalupsky, Albert B.: The reported evaluation of alcoholism treatments, 1968-1971: A methodological review. *Addictive Behaviors, 2*:63-74, 1977.

[23]Crawford and Chalupsky, *Addictive Behaviors,* p. 74.

[24]Crawford and Chalupsky, *Addictive Behaviors,* p. 74.

treatment conditions. Studies by Wallerstein[25] and Ends and Page[26] demonstrate that groups with an untreated status took on a special character on their own and could not be considered a pure control group.

It is imperative that control conditions be established. Practically all studies provide data in which the control condition is not adequate. With this inadequacy present it becomes impossible to isolate the specific variable or variables that may produce the desired outcomes. One example of this situation is given by Alcoholics Anonymous in their book about their organization.[27] A lengthy description of Alcoholics Anonymous and its programs is provided as an indication of its high rate of success. Lacking any control condition one is not quite sure what might account for the reported results.

For Hill and Blane, the key variable to be adequately controlled is motivation for treatment.[28] They report that this variable was not controlled by any study, although the matching groups' effort by Ends and Page and the random assignment of patients to various treatments by Wallerstein succeeded in attempting to control for motivation for treatment. The attempt to establish a control condition prior to the start of these two studies clearly distinguished them from other studies in their literature review.

IDENTIFYING AND DEFINING
THE INDEPENDENT VARIABLE

The independent variable is the specific condition that is supposed to produce a specific outcome. It is most important that these variables be as clearly defined as possible. If this is not adequately done, one will never be able to identify the specific condition being evaluated. For example, it would be necessary to specify the program dimensions which may pro-

[25]Wallerstein, Robert S.: *Hospital Treatment of Alcoholism.* New York, Basic, 1957.
[26]Ends, E. J. and Page, C. W.: A study of three types of group psychotherapy with hospitalized male inebriates. *Quarterly Journal of Studies on Alcohol, 18*:163-277, 1957.
[27]Alcoholics Anonymous: *Alcoholics Anonymous.* New York, Works, 1941.
[28]Hill and Blane, *Quarterly Journal of Studies on Alcohol,* p. 81.

duce the desired treatment outcome. In short, the effort is an attempt to learn what is producing the outcome and why it is occurring.

Clearly defined independent variables allow for others to replicate the study, because identifying the set of conditions makes it possible to reconstruct the same situation. Statements revealing that one group of clients received casework services and another group received casework and group services are totally inadequate because they do not reveal anything definitive about each service. Hence, the same effect cannot be reproduced.

IDENTIFYING AND ISOLATING
THE DEPENDENT VARIABLE

The dependent variable is the desired outcome, and it, too, must be clearly identified and defined. The same reasoning that dominated the attempt to identify independent variables is present in this situation. If the desired outcome is vague, one will never be able to specify what is to be evaluated, nor will one be able to adequately differentiate between independent variables. Many studies use terms such as *sober, improved, moderately improved,* and *unimproved,* without specifying the criterion used to categorize subjects. The terms are vague and are useless to the reader.

The task of identifying the dependent variable in alcoholism and drug research may seem to be somewhat easier than identifying the independent variable. However, the problems in specifying the dependent variable are as complicated and difficult to resolve. In alcoholism research the overwhelming dependent variable is abstinence. A huge majority of evaluation studies on the efficacy of treatment specify abstinence over a period of time as a reliable criterion of successful treatment. Voegtlin and Lemere felt that the treatment of alcoholism lent itself ideally to accurate evaluation and based their evaluative scheme entirely on the abstinence variable.[29]

---

[29]Voegtlin and Lemere, *Quarterly Journal of Studies on Alcohol,* p. 202.

Pattison challenged the religious adherence to abstinence as the desired outcome to be measured. In his critique of alcoholism treatment concepts with special reference to abstinence, he concluded with some tenable statements:

1. Return to normal drinking occurs in a significant portion of treated alcoholics.
2. Improvement in drinking and improvement in social, vocational and psychological adaptation are related but not parallel. Less than total rehabilitation may be the most feasible therapeutic goal in many cases.
3. Abstinence as a necessary condition for successful treatment is an overstatement. It is a prescription which should be used judiciously.
4. Abstinence as a criterion of successful treatment is misleading. It may be maintained at the expense of total life functioning, as in some Alcoholics Anonymous abstainers. Abstinence may also be followed by personality deterioration.
5. The therapeutic efficacy of brief, relatively superficial intervention therapy has been noted. It indicates the need for an evaluation of the nature of the psychodynamic alterations which bring such improvement.[30]

While there appears to be increasing agreement that it is probably more productive and realistic to develop another dependent variable, the problem of clearly specifying that variable might become even more difficult. A clear definition of abstinence has never been achieved as a measure of success, although it is commonly understood to mean to stop drinking. From a research perspective the common definition needs specification.

It is probably more difficult to measure partial improvement in psychosocial functioning or in drinking behavior. Improvement rates in most follow-up studies would undoubtedly increase should partial improvement be accepted as a feasible goal of treatment. The major problem would be in accurately defining and measuring partial improvement.

---

[30]Pattison, *Quarterly Journal of Studies on Alcohol,* p. 66.

PROCEDURE AND MEASUREMENT TECHNIQUE

All studies should clearly delineate all procedures used to secure the data, any measurement techniques, and the statistical techniques used to analyze the data. Lacking specification and clarity, one is placed in a position of assuming that certain procedures were done to insure sound research or that the risks to human subjects were taken into consideration. For example, it would seem important in reporting that certain patients were improved to also note how they were so rated. Definitions of procedures and measurement techniques are described as the study method and, if clear, make it possible for others using the same methods to see if they can produce the same results.

In summary, the state of the art in evaluative research in the drug and particularly the alcohol field continues to be weak. This situation does not make it possible to make definitive statements relative to treatment outcome research. Four major conditions for assessing research competence were presented for use by administrators. Perhaps as they require excellence in research will the state of the art improve.

Chapter 8

CONCLUSION

IT should be clear that the knowledge and the requirements for competent administration of current drug and alcohol programs are more extensive than ever before. Combined with the gap in adequately trained administrators, these two factors make the need for better management important. In the face of public funding and accountability, better management is imperative.

Administration of drug and alcohol programs has been devoted mainly to managing the treatment aspect of separate drug and alcohol programs and not to management issues in administrative practice. Current administrators know the treatment scene well, but if the management perspective continues to exclude the extensive requirements for competent management, the competitive position of the drug and alcohol field in the health and social welfare funding cycle will be weakened.

The text has explored some basic knowledge requirements for competent management of conventional and merged treatment programs. Despite the fairly widespread mixing of drug and alcohol clients in programs, merging has not been given much recognition at the state or federal levels nor in the literature. Merged programs would seem to make sense and when implemented have demonstrated to be helpful to clients. Management of merged treatment programs are also practical with administrative responsibilities basically similar to those in separate drug and alcohol programs.

The substantive chapters on the legal arena, the planning process and fiscal management, social policy issues, and research and evaluation presented the breadth and depth of administrative knowledge in the current scene. The reader is now asked to reflect on these and many other issues relevant to the management process and to rate oneself according to the self-assessment matrix of administrative practice. Administrators should be able to rate themselves with greater accuracy and should notice that their knowledge varies according to the specific issue and the particular subsystem involved. Based on the results obtained from using the self-assessment matrix, administrators can more clearly identify gaps in their knowledge, determine probable difficulties in pursuing certain lines of action, and presumably initiate steps to improve their practice.

Administrators in the drug and alcohol field must continue developing their management skills. They are in a unique position to provide much needed insight and clear reflection to the current state of affairs in the drug and alcohol field. For example, through the use of contracts, administrators can hold researchers accountable for producing quality research, as the current state of the art is quite poor. Perhaps they and the researchers can produce the kind of research that is useful in assessing the efficacy of treatment. After almost seventy years of research in the alcoholism field and about a decade of research in the drug field, there is no hard evidence that counseling makes any difference in rehabilitation.

The legal arena and social policy statements illustrate the ambivalence and ambiguity of public attitude and how quickly laws and policies can change. The increasing alliance between the criminal justice system and the health system should be studied, for it is not clear whether this alliance is in the best interests of the clients or, perhaps more realistically, to what extent clients and their needs are really considered in the field. Indeed, one wonders how clients have benefited by this new alliance or by having their problems diagnosed as medical instead of legal.

Planning can be an extremely valuable technique in administrative practice when used in accordance with certain defined situations. However, planning does have its limitations and is not the panacea for solving some of the more difficult problems confronting administrators. Planning effective programs will not substantially affect the differential attitude of the public toward the variety of available drugs and alcohol. It will not get people jobs nor open other doors in society. Such changes usually happen in a political framework as when DWI laws were instituted or when civil commitment procedures were developed. This is to say also that the drug and alcohol field is perhaps more of a political problem than a medical or legal problem. As Musto states, "the energy that has given impetus to drug control and prohibition came from profound tensions among socioeconomic groups, ethnic minorities and generations — as well as the psychological attraction of certain drugs."[1] If administrators are to have any impact in this field they must recognize the political context in which they operate, one in which poor management practice places them at a distinct disadvantage.

Competent management is as much a function of skill as it is a recognition of need. It is as important to know what one can do as it is to recognize what one cannot do. Knowledge is basic in learning what questions to ask, identifying where assistance in administration would be valuable, and, even more valuable, in pursuing sound administrative action. This is the perspective one can achieve from self-assessment.

Administrative competence is a reasonable expectation which will be achieved only if present methods are changed. Training programs cannot keep pace with the expanding body of administrative knowledge in the drug and alcohol field. Education-oriented programs for administrators would seem to provide an alternative if they would concentrate on helping administrators to conceptually approach management situations. This approach would enable them to determine the reasons for their actions and focus less on how to complete a task using one method. If administrators could determine for themselves the value of a generic fiscal management program, they would take the development of each new technique in stride. Administrators would be acting in response to perceived administrative need rather than reacting to external regulatory demands.

In a sense there is no conclusion to this book. Completion of the text provides a basis for evaluating one's knowledge in administration of a drug and alcohol program. A successful

---

[1]Musto, David F.: *The American Disease: Origins of Narcotic Control.* New Haven, Ct., Yale Univ. Press, 1973, p. 244.

conclusion rests in administrators turning gained knowledge into action. This is a continuing task but one in which education can serve a useful purpose. The time has come for better management to no longer be a major problem in the rehabilitation of those suffering from drug or alcohol addiction. The major thrust and emphasis needs to be directed toward successful rehabilitative efforts. This task is formidable indeed; it needs to be supported by competent management.

INDEX